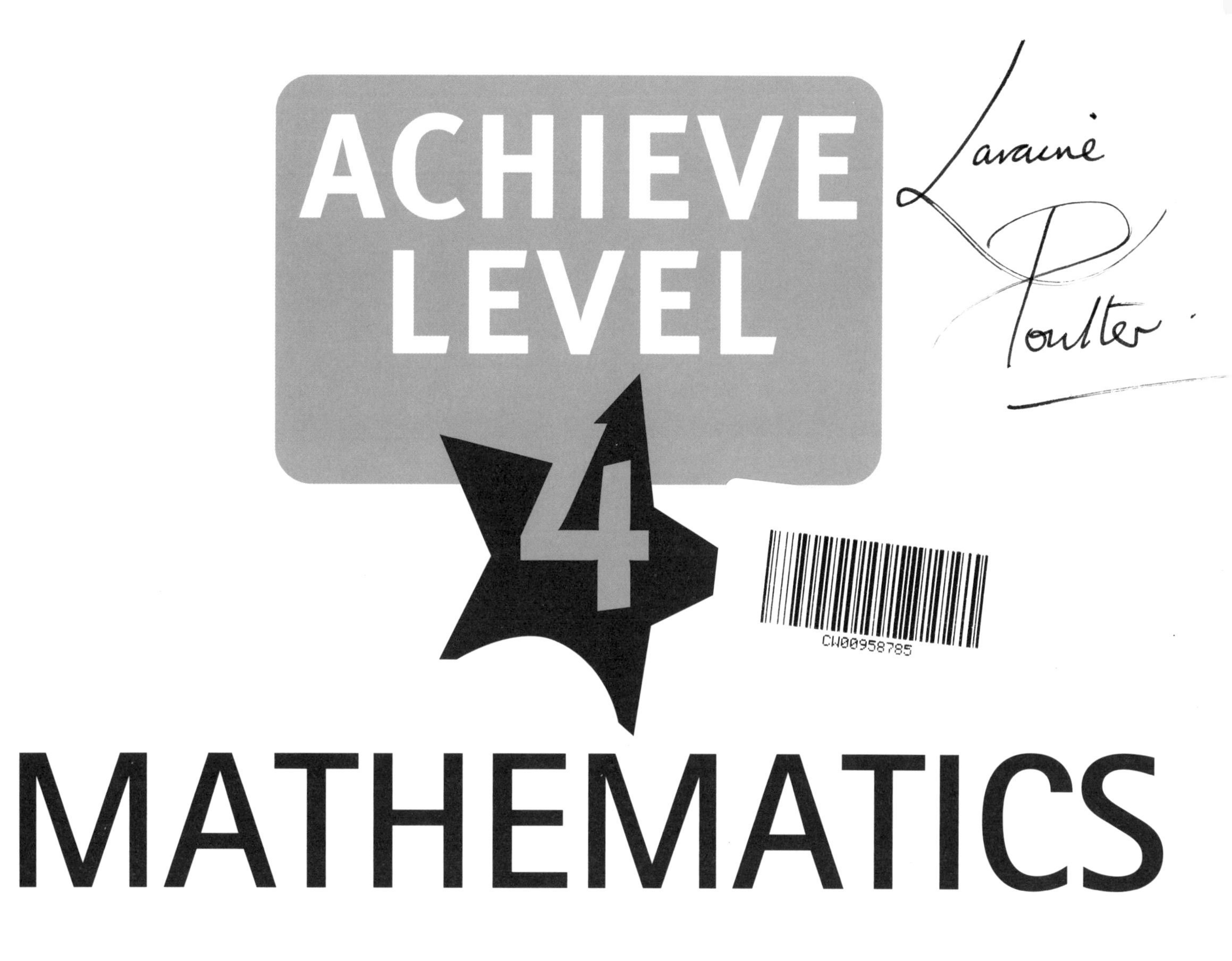

By **Richard Cooper**

Rising Stars UK Ltd, 76 Farnaby Road, Bromley, BR1 4BH
www.risingstars-uk.com

Published 2003
New Edition 2003
Reprinted 2004 (three times), 2005
New full colour edition 2005

Design: Branford Graphics
Illustrations: Burville Riley, Beehive Illustration (Theresa Tibbetts) and Ken Vail Graphic Design
Cover image: Beehive Illustration (Theresa Tibbetts)
Cover design: Burville Riley

British Library Cataloguing in Publication Data
A CIP record for this book is available from the British Library.

ISBN: 1-905056-00-1

Printed by Craft Print International Ltd, Singapore

Contents

How to use this book

1. **Introduction section** – This section tells you what you need to do to get a Level 4. It picks out the key learning objective and explains it simply to you.

2. **Self assessment** – Colour in the face that best describes your understanding of this concept.

3. **Question** – The question helps you to learn by doing. It is presented in a similar way to a SATs question and gives you a real example to work with.

4. **Flow chart** – This shows you the steps to use when completing questions like this.

   This icon indicates the section is a *teaching* section.

5. **Tip boxes** – These provide test hints and general tips on getting the best marks in the SATs.

What we have included:

Those topics at Level 3 that are trickiest to get right.
ALL Level 4 content so you know that you are covering all the topics that could come up in the test.

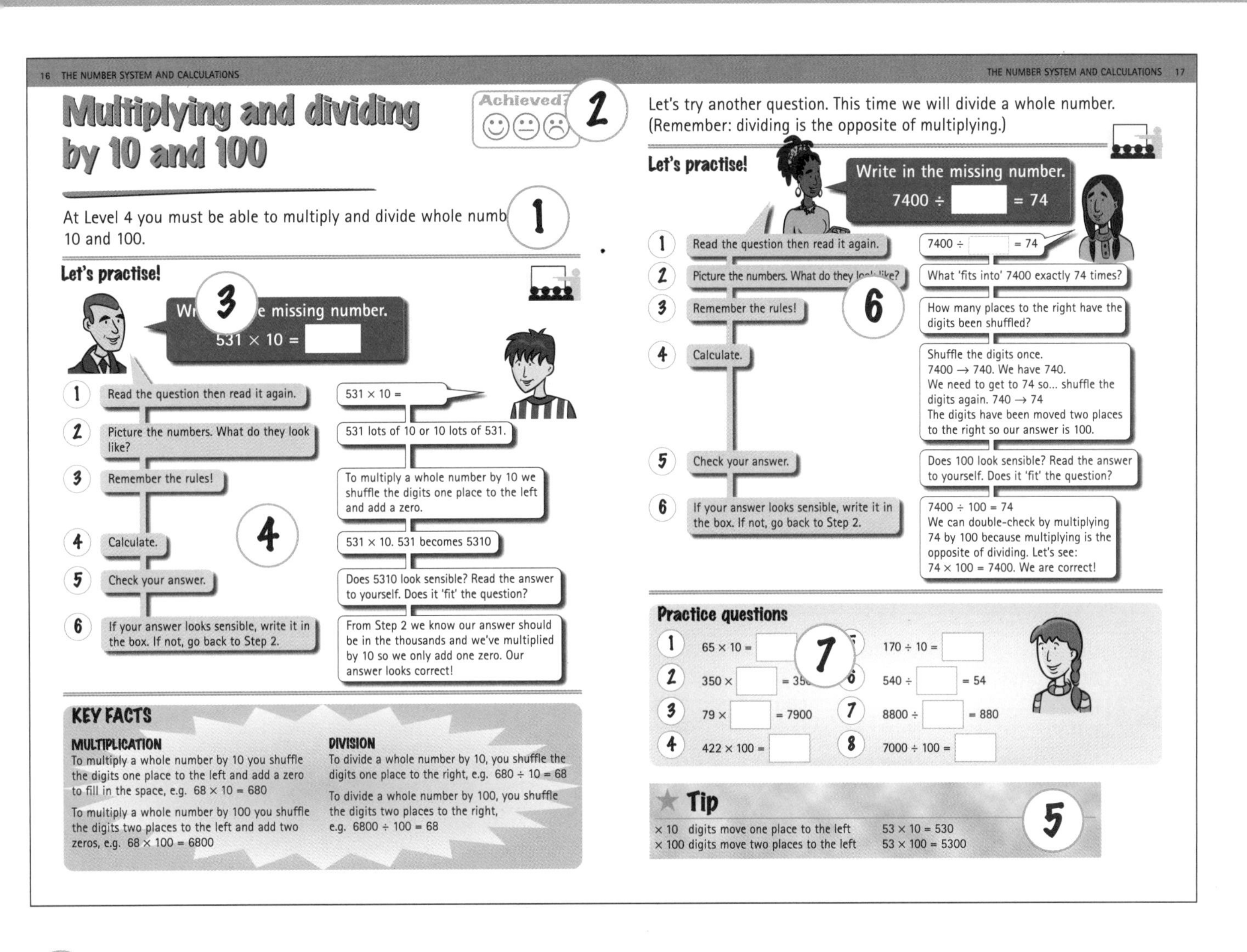

16 THE NUMBER SYSTEM AND CALCULATIONS

Multiplying and dividing by 10 and 100

Achieved?

At Level 4 you must be able to multiply and divide whole numb 10 and 100.

Let's practise!

e missing number. 531 × 10 =

1	Read the question then read it again.	531 × 10 =
2	Picture the numbers. What do they look like?	531 lots of 10 or 10 lots of 531.
3	Remember the rules!	To multiply a whole number by 10 we shuffle the digits one place to the left and add a zero.
4	Calculate.	531 × 10. 531 becomes 5310
5	Check your answer.	Does 5310 look sensible? Read the answer to yourself. Does it 'fit' the question?
6	If your answer looks sensible, write it in the box. If not, go back to Step 2.	From Step 2 we know our answer should be in the thousands and we've multiplied by 10 so we only add one zero. Our answer looks correct!

KEY FACTS

MULTIPLICATION

To multiply a whole number by 10 you shuffle the digits one place to the left and add a zero to fill in the space, e.g. 68 × 10 = 680

To multiply a whole number by 100 you shuffle the digits two places to the left and add two zeros, e.g. 68 × 100 = 6800

DIVISION

To divide a whole number by 10, you shuffle the digits one place to the right, e.g. 680 ÷ 10 = 68

To divide a whole number by 100, you shuffle the digits two places to the right, e.g. 6800 ÷ 100 = 68

THE NUMBER SYSTEM AND CALCULATIONS 17

Let's try another question. This time we will divide a whole number. (Remember: dividing is the opposite of multiplying.)

Let's practise!

Write in the missing number. 7400 ÷ ☐ = 74

1	Read the question then read it again.	7400 ÷ ☐ = 74
2	Picture the numbers. What do they look like?	What 'fits into' 7400 exactly 74 times?
3	Remember the rules!	How many places to the right have the digits been shuffled?
4	Calculate.	Shuffle the digits once. 7400 → 740. We have 740. We need to get to 74 so... shuffle the digits again. 740 → 74 The digits have been moved two places to the right so our answer is 100.
5	Check your answer.	Does 100 look sensible? Read the answer to yourself. Does it 'fit' the question?
6	If your answer looks sensible, write it in the box. If not, go back to Step 2.	7400 ÷ 100 = 74 We can double-check by multiplying 74 by 100 because multiplying is the opposite of dividing. Let's see: 74 × 100 = 7400. We are correct!

Practice questions

1. 65 × 10 =
2. 350 × ☐ = 35
3. 79 × ☐ = 7900
4. 422 × 100 =
5. 170 ÷ 10 =
6. 540 ÷ ☐ = 54
7. 8800 ÷ ☐ = 880
8. 7000 ÷ 100 =

Tip

× 10 digits move one place to the left 53 × 10 = 530

× 100 digits move two places to the left 53 × 100 = 5300

6 **Second question** – On most pages there will be a second question. This will either look at a slightly different question type or give you another example to work through.

7 **Practice questions** – This is where you have to do the work! Try the question using the technique in the flow chart then check your answers at the back. Practising questions is the best way to help improve your understanding.

We have also put in a big selection of our favourite test techniques, tips for revision and some advice on what the National Tests are all about, as well as the answers so you can see how well you are getting on.

GOOD LUCK!

Achieve Level 4 Maths – Objectives

This chart allows you to see which objectives in the National Numeracy Strategy have been covered and which are to be completed.

We have matched the objectives directly with each page of Achieve Level 4 so you can monitor progress.

When children have indicated 'achievement', you can encourage them to tick the box or highlight that row in this table. That way, you and your class know what has been achieved and what is still to be covered.

Text in **bold** denotes key objectives.

Page no.	Title	Objective	Achieved?
Level 3 – The Tricky Bits			
8	Decimal notation and negative numbers	Understand decimal notation and place value for tenths and hundredths and use them in context Recognise negative numbers in context (Numbers and the Number System)	
9	Subtraction	**Develop and refine written methods for column subtraction of two whole numbers less than 1000** (Calculations)	
10	2, 3, 4, 5 and 10 times tables	**Know by heart multiplication facts for 2, 3, 4, 5 and 10 times tables** (Calculations)	
11	Number problems	Solve mathematical problems or puzzles, recognise patterns and relationships, generalise and predict (Solving Problems)	
12	Equivalent fractions	**Recognise the equivalence of simple fractions** (Numbers and the Number System)	
13	Classifying 3D and 2D shapes	Classify and describe 3D and 2D shapes, referring to properties such as reflective symmetry (2D), the number or shapes of faces, the number of sides/edges and vertices, whether sides/edges are the same length, whether or not angles are right angles (Measures, Shapes and Space)	
14	Tables and lists	**Solve a given problem by organising and interpreting numerical data in simple lists, tables and graphs** (Handling Data)	
15	Bar charts and pictograms	**Solve a given problem by organising and interpreting numerical data in simple lists, tables and graphs** (Handling Data)	
The Number System and Calculations			
16–17	Multiplying and dividing by 10 and 100	**Multiply and divide decimals by 10 or 100, and integers by 1000, and explain effect**	
18	Short addition	**Extend written methods to column addition of two integers less than 10,000; addition of more than two integers less than 10,000**	
19	Short subtraction	**Extend written methods to column subtraction of two integers less than 10,000**; subtraction of more than two integers less than 10,000	
20–21	Decimals	Use decimal notation for tenths and hundredths **Extend written methods to column addition and subtraction of numbers involving decimals** **Order a mixed set of numbers** or measurements **with up to three decimal places**	
22	Short multiplication	Approximate first. Use informal pencil and paper methods to support, record or explain multiplications **Extend written methods to short multiplication of HTU by U**	
23	Short division	Approximate first. Use informal pencil and paper methods to support, record or explain divisions Extend written methods to short division of HTU by U (with integer remainder)	

24–25	Recognising proportions of a whole	**Relate fractions to their decimal representations** Express one half, one quarter, three quarters, and tenths and hundredths, as percentages Find fractions of numbers or quantities Understand and find percentages of small whole number quantities	
26–27	Number patterns	Recognise and extend number sequences formed by counting from any number in steps of constant size, extending beyond zero when counting back Find all the pairs of factors of any number up to 100 Recognise prime numbers up to at least 20 Recognise multiples up to 10 × 10. Know and apply simple tests of divisibility. Find simple common multiples	
28–29	Checking your answers	Check with the inverse operation when using a calculator Check the sum of several numbers by adding in the reverse order Check with an equivalent calculation Estimate by approximating (round to nearest 10 or 100) then check result Use knowledge of sums and differences of odd/even numbers	
Measures, Shape and Space			
30–31	Using coordinates	Read and plot coordinates in all four quadrants. Recognise position and direction	
32–33	3D shapes – making models	Visualise 3D shapes from 2D drawings and identify different nets for an open cube	
34–35	2D shapes	**Recognise properties of rectangles** Classify triangles using criteria such as equal sides, equal angles, lines of symmetry Recognise where a shape will be after reflection in a mirror line parallel to one side (sides not all parallel, or perpendicular to the mirror line) Make shapes with increasing accuracy	
36	Finding the perimeters of simple shapes	**Calculate the perimeter of simple compound shapes that can be split into rectangles** **Understand area measured in square centimetres** Measure and calculate the area of shapes using counting methods	
37	Finding areas of shapes by counting	Measure and calculate the area of rectangles and other simple shapes using counting methods and standard units (cm^2)	
38	Measures	Suggest suitable units and measuring equipment to estimate or measure length, mass or capacity	
39	Reading scales	Record estimates and readings from scales to a suitable degree of accuracy	
Handling Data			
40–41	Grouping data	**Solve a problem** by representing, **extracting and interpreting data in tables, graphs and charts** and diagrams, including those generated by a computer	
42	Finding the range	Finding the range of a set of data	
43	Finding the mode	Find the mode of a set of data	
44–45	Line graphs	Solve a problem by representing, extracting and interpreting data in tables and graphs, including those generated by a computer	
Solving Problems			
46–47	Using simple formulae	Make and investigate a general statement about familiar numbers or shapes by finding examples that satisfy it. Develop from explaining a generalised relationship in words to expressing it in a formula using letters as symbols	
Using and Applying Mathematics			
48–57	Using and applying mathematics – solving problems	Choose and use appropriate number operations to solve problems and appropriate ways of calculating: mental, mental with jottings, written methods, calculator Explain methods and reasoning, orally and in writing Solve mathematical problems or puzzles, recognise and explain patterns and relationships, generalise and predict **Identify and use appropriate operations (including combinations of operations) to solve word problems involving numbers and quantities** based on 'real life', money or measures, using one or more steps **Explain methods and reasoning**	

Decimal notation and negative numbers

Money

A good way to understand more about decimals is to work with money. We use pounds and pence. There are one hundred pence in one pound.

We use 'decimal notation' to record money.

Three pounds fifty pence is written like this.

On the left of the decimal point is the number of whole pounds.

On the right of the decimal point is the number of pence or fractions of a whole pound.

number of pounds
number of pence

£3.50

pound sign
decimal point separating pounds and pence

For each of these amounts, write the number of pounds and number of pence.

1. £7.42
   ________ pounds
   ________ pence
2. £14.28
   ________ pounds
   ________ pence
3. £53.71
   ________ pounds
   ________ pence
4. £109.86
   ________ pounds
   ________ pence
5. £426.19
   ________ pounds
   ________ pence

Temperature

Negative numbers are numbers below zero. Thermometers measure temperature and use numbers below zero when it is freezing (0°).

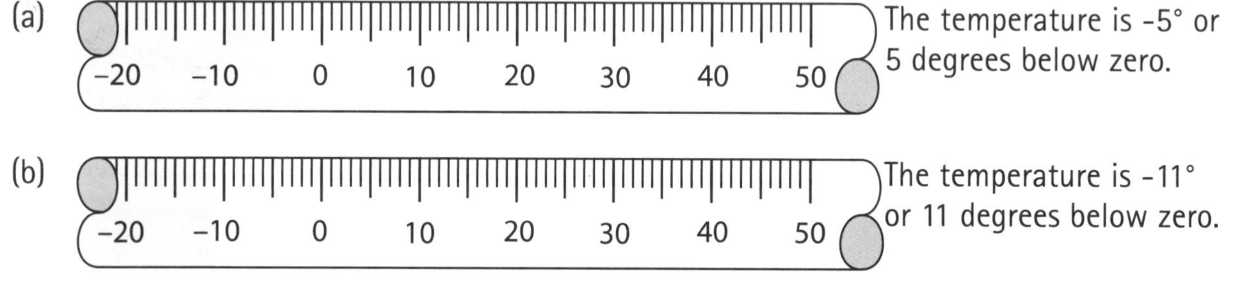

(a) The temperature is -5° or 5 degrees below zero.

(b) The temperature is -11° or 11 degrees below zero.

Which do you think is colder? (a) ☐ (b) ☐

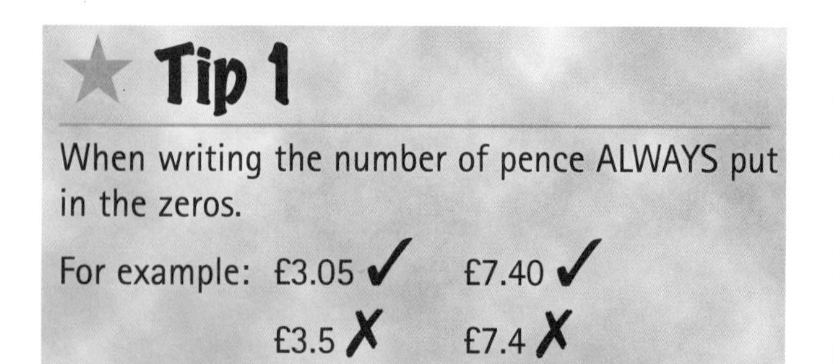

Tip 1

When writing the number of pence ALWAYS put in the zeros.

For example: £3.05 ✓ £7.40 ✓

£3.5 ✗ £7.4 ✗

Tip 2

Don't forget to include zero when counting up and down a temperature scale.
Think of a thermometer like a number line.
The greater the negative number on a thermometer, the colder it is.

Subtraction

Written subtractions

You will be able to do some sums easily in your head (e.g. 200 – 100). Others are a bit harder and you may need a paper and pencil.

Let's practise!

Write in the missing number.

749 – 365 = ☐

1. Estimate first. — 750 – 350. Our answer will be around 400.
2. Write the digits neatly in their columns.

```
  H T U
  7 4 9
- 3 6 5
-------
```

3. Start with the units, then the tens, then the hundreds. If the top number is smaller than the bottom number, then exchange across from the next column.

```
   H T U
  ⁶7̸ ¹4 9
-  3  6 5
---------
      8 4
```

In the tens column, the top number (4) is smaller than the bottom number (6) so we need to exchange from the hundreds column. 14 – 6 = 8

4. Now do the digits in the hundreds column to complete your answer.

```
   H T U
  ⁶7̸ ¹4 9
-  3  6 5
---------
   3  8 4
```

6 – 3 = 3

5. Does your answer look sensible? — Yes, the estimate was 400.

Practice questions

Try these. Round up or down to estimate your answer first.

1. 443 – 372 = ☐
2. 795 – 628 = ☐
3. 482 – 336 = ☐
4. 910 – 772 = ☐
5. 835 – 671 = ☐
6. 655 – 556 = ☐

★ Tip

Work step-by-step starting with the units and work towards the left hand side.

★ Tip

Don't forget that you can check the answer to a subtraction by using addition.

2, 3, 4, 5 and 10 times tables

To achieve Level 4 you will need to know and be able to use all these table facts.

2 times table	3 times table	4 times table	5 times table	10 times table
$1 \times 2 = 2$	$1 \times 3 = 3$	$1 \times 4 = 4$	$1 \times 5 = 5$	$1 \times 10 = 10$
$2 \times 2 = 4$	$2 \times 3 = 6$	$2 \times 4 = 8$	$2 \times 5 = 10$	$2 \times 10 = 20$
$3 \times 2 = 6$	$3 \times 3 = 9$	$3 \times 4 = 12$	$3 \times 5 = 15$	$3 \times 10 = 30$
$4 \times 2 = 8$	$4 \times 3 = 12$	$4 \times 4 = 16$	$4 \times 5 = 20$	$4 \times 10 = 40$
$5 \times 2 = 10$	$5 \times 3 = 15$	$5 \times 4 = 20$	$5 \times 5 = 25$	$5 \times 10 = 50$
$6 \times 2 = 12$	$6 \times 3 = 18$	$6 \times 4 = 24$	$6 \times 5 = 30$	$6 \times 10 = 60$
$7 \times 2 = 14$	$7 \times 3 = 21$	$7 \times 4 = 28$	$7 \times 5 = 35$	$7 \times 10 = 70$
$8 \times 2 = 16$	$8 \times 3 = 24$	$8 \times 4 = 32$	$8 \times 5 = 40$	$8 \times 10 = 80$
$9 \times 2 = 18$	$9 \times 3 = 27$	$9 \times 4 = 36$	$9 \times 5 = 45$	$9 \times 10 = 90$
$10 \times 2 = 20$	$10 \times 3 = 30$	$10 \times 4 = 40$	$10 \times 5 = 50$	$10 \times 10 = 100$

Tip 1
Answers are always even numbers.

Tip 2
The digits, when added together, make 3, 6 or 9.

Tip 3
The answers are double the 2 times table.

Tip 4
The answers always end in 5 or 0.

Tip 5
The answers always end in 0.

Using tables facts to help with division sums

Remember, division is the **inverse** or **opposite** of multiplication. For example:

$$5 \times 4 = 20 \text{ so } 20 \div 4 = 5$$

Practice questions

Use the multiplication tables to complete these division facts.

1. $12 \div 6 =$ ☐
2. $28 \div 4 =$ ☐
3. ☐ $\div 7 = 10$
4. $36 \div 4 =$ ☐
5. $25 \div$ ☐ $= 5$
6. ☐ $\div 2 = 7$
7. $16 \div$ ☐ $= 2$
8. ☐ $\div 10 = 8$
9. $36 \div 6 =$ ☐
10. ☐ $\div 4 = 8$
11. $40 \div$ ☐ $= 8$
12. $20 \div 4 =$ ☐
13. ☐ $\div 2 = 3$
14. $4 \div 4 =$ ☐
15. $21 \div 3 =$ ☐

Number problems

Number problems often 'hide' the maths behind the words.
Follow our step-by-step guide to achieve success!

Let's practise!

Harvey has 4 football stickers. Oona has 6 times as many football stickers as Harvey. How many stickers does Oona have?

1. Read the question then read it again.
2. Picture the numbers.
3. Decide which operation to use and calculate.
4. Read the question and answer. What were you asked to do? Is your answer sensible?

This is really important. There are lots of words in this question.

4 6

6 times as many
That means multiply ...
Harvey has 4 stickers so $4 \times 6 = 24$.

How many stickers does Oona have?
Oona has 24 stickers.

Number problems involving division might not have answers that fit exactly. They may have remainders. You have to decide whether to round the answer up or down.

Miss Banks has 29 children in her class. A table seats 4 children. How many tables does she need to seat all the children?

1. Read the question then read it again.
2. Picture the numbers.
3. Decide which operation to use and calculate.
4. Round up or round down?

How many tables to seat the children?
It's division. $29 \div 4 = 7$ r1

Up... so 8 tables are needed to seat all the children. Otherwise 1 would be standing.

Equivalent fractions

To achieve Level 4 you will need to be able to use fractions that are parts of a whole and recognise when two fractions are equivalent.

KEY FACTS A fraction is 'part of a number'.

A quarter or $\frac{1}{4}$ means 1 part out of 4 equal parts. One quarter of this diagram has been shaded.

Three quarters or $\frac{3}{4}$ means 3 parts out of 4 equal parts. Three quarters of this diagram have been shaded.

Have a look at this group of marbles.

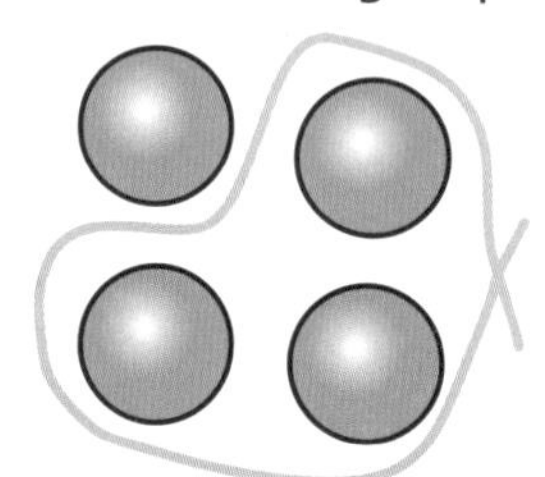

What fraction is circled? Answer $\frac{3}{4}$ or 'three quarters'.

What fraction is not circled? Answer $\frac{1}{4}$ or 'one quarter'.

Try this question.

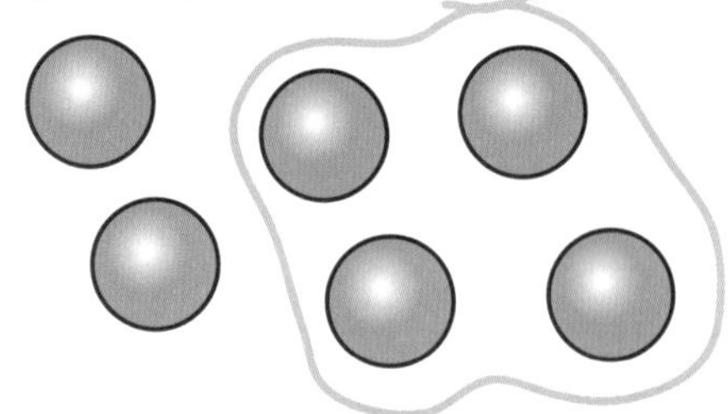

What fraction is circled? Answer

What fraction is not circled? Answer

Equivalent fractions are the same, even though they look different from each other.

Eating $\frac{2}{4}$ of a cake is **the same as** or **equivalent** to eating half of the cake.

Look back at the marbles questions. Using this equivalent fractions chart, can you see what fractions your answers are the same as?

1							
$\frac{1}{2}$	$\frac{1}{2}$						
$\frac{1}{3}$	$\frac{1}{3}$	$\frac{1}{3}$					
$\frac{1}{4}$	$\frac{1}{4}$	$\frac{1}{4}$	$\frac{1}{4}$				
$\frac{1}{5}$	$\frac{1}{5}$	$\frac{1}{5}$	$\frac{1}{5}$	$\frac{1}{5}$			
$\frac{1}{6}$	$\frac{1}{6}$	$\frac{1}{6}$	$\frac{1}{6}$	$\frac{1}{6}$	$\frac{1}{6}$		
$\frac{1}{7}$	$\frac{1}{7}$	$\frac{1}{7}$	$\frac{1}{7}$	$\frac{1}{7}$	$\frac{1}{7}$	$\frac{1}{7}$	
$\frac{1}{8}$	$\frac{1}{8}$	$\frac{1}{8}$	$\frac{1}{8}$	$\frac{1}{8}$	$\frac{1}{8}$	$\frac{1}{8}$	$\frac{1}{8}$

Look at one half ($\frac{1}{2}$). Can you see that it is the same as or equivalent to: $\frac{2}{4}$, $\frac{3}{6}$, $\frac{4}{8}$?

Study the chart to find more equivalent fractions. Write two here:

[ ] is the same as [ ]   [ ] is the same as [ ]

Classifying 3D and 2D shapes

3D (three dimensional) shapes

3D shapes are solid shapes. When looking at pictures of 3D shapes you have to imagine the bits you can't 'see'.

This picture of a cube shows 3 faces but of course there are actually 6!

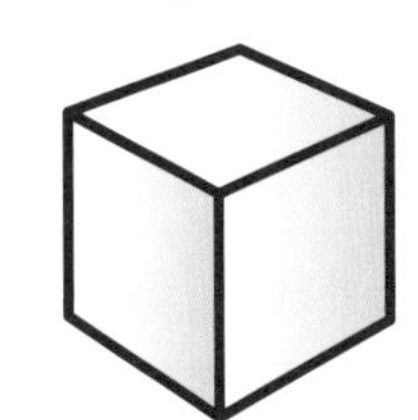

Here are some names of 3D shapes.

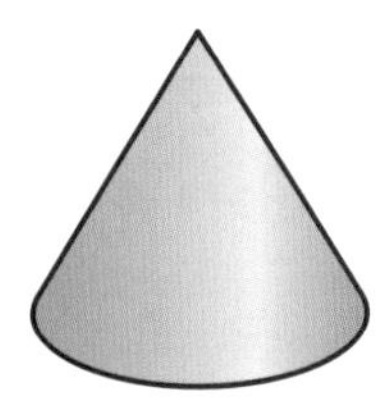

Cone

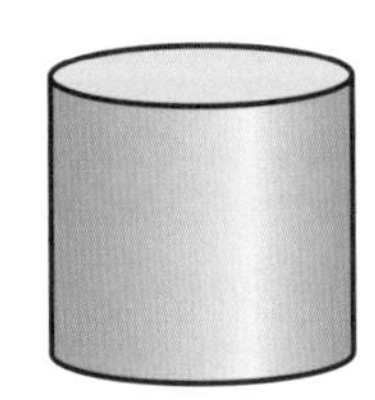

Cylinder

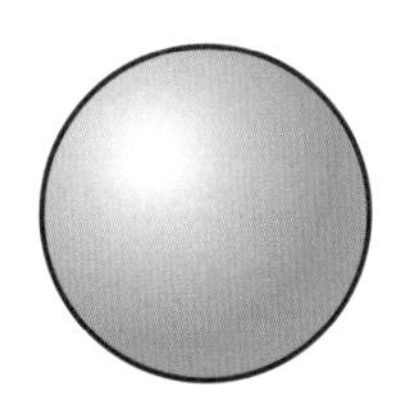

Sphere

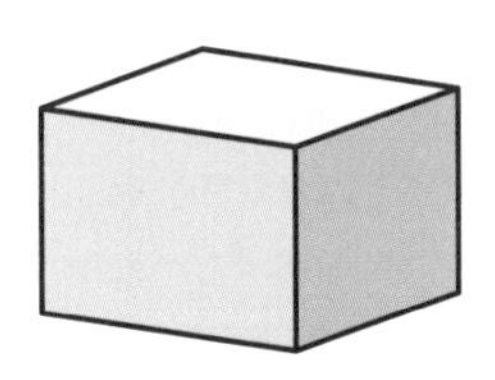

Cuboid

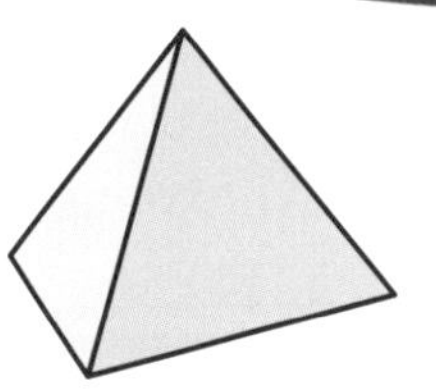

Triangular-based pyramid

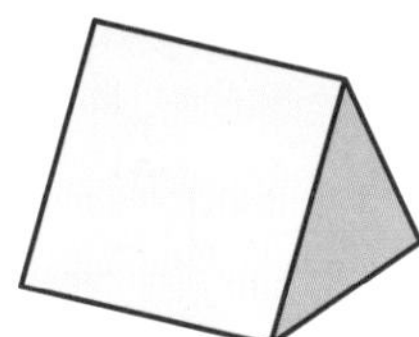

Triangular prism

3D shapes are made up of faces, edges and vertices.

- A face is a flat surface of a solid shape.
- An edge is where two faces meet at an angle.
- A vertex is where 3 or more edges meet – a corner.

Complete this chart to help you to understand more about 3D shapes. If you don't have the shapes in front of you, try to picture them in your mind.

	Cone	Cylinder	Sphere	Cuboid	Triangular-based pyramid	Triangular prism
Number of faces						
Number of edges						
Number of vertices						

2D (two dimensional) shapes

2D shapes are 'flat shapes'. If they have straight sides they are called polygons. If they have straight sides and all the angles and sides are equal they are called regular polygons.

Symmetry

A shape is symmetrical (has symmetry) if both sides are the same when a mirror line is drawn. This is also called 'reflective symmetry'.
Take a look:

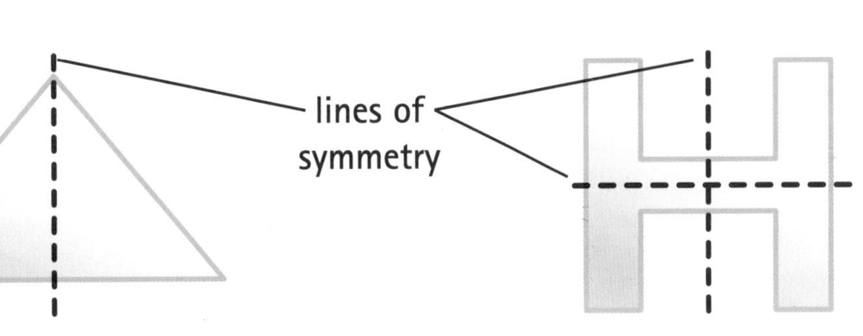

Tables and lists

In mathematics, information can be presented to you in many different ways. The key to getting a Level 4 is to work out what the graph, table or list is trying to tell you and then answer the questions.

This step-by-step guide will help you to score maximum points on Handling Data questions.

1. Read the question then read it again.

   There is always a lot of information in these questions. Some you need and some you don't. Always read and think carefully.

2. Look for key words and phrases in the questions.

   Make sure you understand what you are being asked to find out.

3. Use your finger or a pencil to follow along the rows or down the columns.

   When you think you've found the information you need, read the question again to double-check.

4. Look back to the question and then read your answer. Does it make sense?

   If it does, write in your answer. If not go back to Step 1.

Practice questions

Here is a table about three children in a Year 5 class.

Like playing with	Jessica	Enya	Thomas
CHAVZ! dolls	✗	✗	✓
Toy truck	✓	✓	✗
My Little T-Rex	✓	✗	✓
The dog	✗	✓	✗
Justin from Year 6	✓	✓	✓

Read the table. Answer these questions.

1. Who doesn't like my Little T-Rex?

   ____

2. Who likes toy trucks?

   ____

3. Who doesn't like playing with the dog?

   ____

Tip

Key words and phrases might include:

How many... Who... What is... Where can you find...
Which one... When does... When can... What comes after...

Bar charts and pictograms

When you are reading charts and graphs it is important to have a system so that you can interpret the information accurately. Follow this step-by-step approach and you won't go wrong!

1. Read the information then read it again. — Include the title. What is the graph or chart trying to tell you?
2. Look to see what each axis (or each pictogram) represents.
3. Look at the scale or the numbers going up the side of the graph (the *y* axis). See how much each symbol, or pictogram, is worth. — Do the numbers go up in 1s, 2s, 5s or 10s? If one picture is worth 2 sandwiches, for example, what is half a picture worth?
4. Look at each bar. Read across the scale and work out the amounts. For pictograms, add up the number of symbols for each category. — Make sure you are accurate. Use your finger or a ruler and ALWAYS double-check your final answer.

Practice questions

Here is a bar chart showing the favourite sandwich fillings in Year 6.

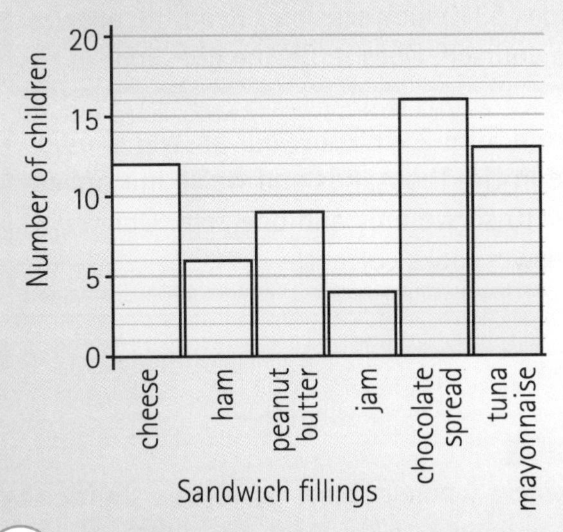

Here is the same information in a pictogram. A pictogram uses symbols to show a group of units.

cheese

ham

peanut butter

jam

chocolate spread

tuna mayonnaise

= 2 children

= 1 child

1. Which is the second most popular filling? ________________
2. How many more children like chocolate spread than peanut butter? ________________
3. How many children in total like cheese and ham fillings? ________________

Multiplying and dividing by 10 and 100

At Level 4 you must be able to multiply and divide whole numbers by 10 and 100.

Let's practise!

Write in the missing number.

$531 \times 10 = \square$

1. Read the question then read it again.

$531 \times 10 =$

2. Picture the numbers. What do they look like?

531 lots of 10 or 10 lots of 531.

3. Remember the rules!

To multiply a whole number by 10 we shuffle the digits one place to the left and add a zero.

4. Calculate.

531×10. 531 becomes 5310

5. Check your answer.

Does 5310 look sensible? Read the answer to yourself. Does it 'fit' the question?

6. If your answer looks sensible, write it in the box. If not, go back to Step 2.

From Step 2 we know our answer should be in the thousands and we've multiplied by 10 so we only add one zero. Our answer looks correct!

KEY FACTS

MULTIPLICATION

To multiply a whole number by 10 you shuffle the digits one place to the left and add a zero to fill in the space, e.g. $68 \times 10 = 680$

To multiply a whole number by 100 you shuffle the digits two places to the left and add two zeros, e.g. $68 \times 100 = 6800$

DIVISION

To divide a whole number by 10, you shuffle the digits one place to the right, e.g. $680 \div 10 = 68$

To divide a whole number by 100, you shuffle the digits two places to the right, e.g. $6800 \div 100 = 68$

Let's try another question. This time we will divide a whole number. (Remember: dividing is the opposite of multiplying.)

Let's practise!

Write in the missing number.

$7400 \div \square = 74$

1. Read the question then read it again. — $7400 \div \square = 74$
2. Picture the numbers. What do they look like? — What 'fits into' 7400 exactly 74 times?
3. Remember the rules! — How many places to the right have the digits been shuffled?
4. Calculate. — Shuffle the digits once. $7400 \rightarrow 740$. We have 740. We need to get to 74 so... shuffle the digits again. $740 \rightarrow 74$ The digits have been moved two places to the right so our answer is 100.
5. Check your answer. — Does 100 look sensible? Read the answer to yourself. Does it 'fit' the question?
6. If your answer looks sensible, write it in the box. If not, go back to Step 2. — $7400 \div 100 = 74$ We can double-check by multiplying 74 by 100 because multiplying is the opposite of dividing. Let's see: $74 \times 100 = 7400$. We are correct!

Practice questions

1. $65 \times 10 = \square$

2. $350 \times \square = 3500$
3. $79 \times \square = 7900$
4. $422 \times 100 = \square$
5. $170 \div 10 = \square$
6. $540 \div \square = 54$
7. $8800 \div \square = 880$
8. $7000 \div 100 = \square$

Tip

$\times$ 10 digits move one place to the left — $53 \times 10 = 530$

$\times$ 100 digits move two places to the left — $53 \times 100 = 5300$

Short addition

To achieve a Level 4 you will need to add and subtract numbers with digits in the thousands, hundreds, tens and units.

Let's practise!

What is the total of these numbers?

52, 612, 8, 2127

1. Read the question then read it again.
   "total of"... It's an addition sum.
2. Picture the numbers. Estimate an answer.
   Round the numbers and estimate: 50 + 600 + 10 + 2100 = 2760
3. Line up the digits in the correct columns.

	Th	H	T	U
	2	1	2	7
		6	1	2
			5	2
+				8

4. Add up the right hand (units) column. Any total over 9, carry the tens digit to the next column.

	Th	H	T	U
	2	1	2	7
		6	1	2
			5	2
+				8
				9
			1	

5. Repeat with the tens column, remembering to carry any totals over 9. Repeat again with the hundreds and thousands columns.

	Th	H	T	U
	2	1	2	7
		6	1	2
			5	2
+				8
	2	7	9	9
			1	

6. Check your answer against your estimate. Does it look right? If not go back to Step 2.
   Our estimate was 2760. We were very close with 2799!

Practice questions

1. Find the sum of 523, 24, 7946.
2. Add together 6, 17, 87 and 789.
3. Increase 743 by 1328 and then add 9.
4. Add 3153 to 8826.

Short subtraction

Now let's try a subtraction question.

Let's practise!

Find the difference between 4734 and 497.

1. Read the question then read it again.

   "find the difference between"... It's a subtraction sum.

2. Picture the numbers. Estimate an answer.

   Round the numbers and estimate: 4700 – 500 = 4200

3. Line up the digits in the correct columns.

```
Th H T U
 4 7 3 4
-  4 9 7
--------

--------
```

4. Start with the right hand (units) column and subtract the bottom number from the top. If the bottom number is bigger then 'exchange' a ten from the tens.

```
Th H T U
     2 1
 4 7 3 4
-  4 9 7
--------
       7
--------
```

5. Repeat with the tens column, remembering to exchange if the bottom number is bigger than the top number. Repeat with the hundreds and then the thousands.

```
Th H T U
   6 12 1
 4 7 3 4
-  4 9 7
--------
 4 2 3 7
--------
```

6. Check your answer against your estimate. Does it look right? If not go back to Step 2.

   Our estimate was 4200. Pretty close to the right answer! That's great.

Practice questions

1. How much less than 8468 is 517? ☐
2. Decrease 6624 by 436. ☐
3. What is 8396 minus 436? ☐
4. Take away 1143 from 3668. ☐

Decimals

Decimals are not whole numbers, e.g. the decimal 3.8 is 'in between' 3 and 4. We say it as '3 point 8'. Let's look at 3.8 on this number line.

0 1 2 3 3.8↓ 4 5 6

When we add or subtract decimals we need to make sure that we line up the decimal points. Money is written using decimals, e.g. 3.8 would be £3.80.

7.92 kg + 7.16 kg + 4.3 kg = ☐

1. Read the question then read it again.
2. Picture the numbers. What do they look like?
   - 7.92 is nearly 8
     7.16 is just over 7
     4.3 is just over 4
3. Study the numbers and think about them! Estimate your answer.
   - 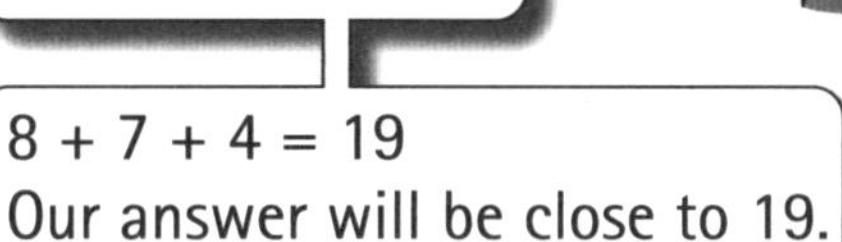
     8 + 7 + 4 = 19
     Our answer will be close to 19.
4. Remember the rule! When adding or subtracting decimals, line up the decimal points. Calculate.
   - 7.92
     7.16
     4.30
     19.38
     Add a zero to 4.3 to make them all the same length. Start by adding up the right hand column. Work towards the left.
5. Does your answer look sensible? Check back to your estimate in Step 3.
   - 19.38 is close to our estimate of 19.
6. If your answer looks sensible, write it in the box. If not, go back to Step 2.
   - Yes, our answer of 19.38 kg looks sensible. Always remember to put the units of measurement on your final answer.

Practice questions

Use the flow chart to work out these additions.

1. 6.34 + 8.77 ☐
2. 67.5 km + 55.8 km ☐
3.  £6.67 + £7.26 + £1.99 ☐

Find the difference between these numbers.

4. 19.22 and 27.78 ☐
5. 27.4 and 28.68 ☐
6.  93.29 km and 54.45 km ☐

Let's try a simple question about ordering decimals.

These are the distances jumped in the long jump competition at the school sports day by class 6C.

Keeley 3.65 m	Dominic 2.73 m	Harry 2.79 m
Jamie 3.75 m	Ellie 3.3 m	Seniz 2.7 m

Write down the distances in order of size, starting with the furthest jump.

1st ________ 2nd ________ 3rd ________

4th ________ 5th ________ 6th ________

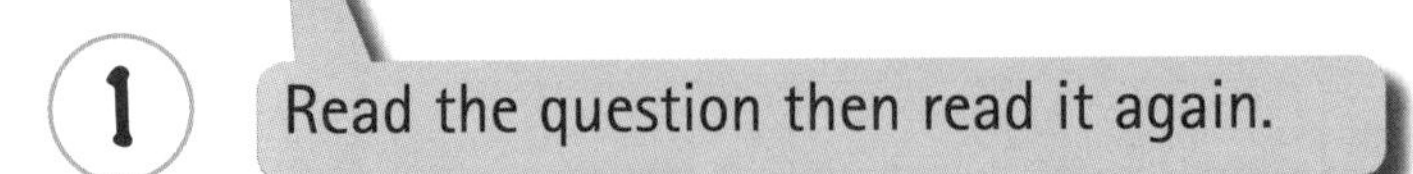

1. Read the question then read it again.

   Lots of words as well as numbers. Be careful! 'Furthest' means highest number.

2. Write the numbers down underneath each other and line up the decimal points.

   3.65
   2.73
   2.79
   3.75
   3.30 Add a zero to 3.3 and 2.7 to
   3.70 make them all the same length.

3. Starting from the top, order the numbers, highest first.

   Working downwards, which is the highest? 3.75 then 3.65...

4. Continue until all the numbers have been ordered.

   Now 3.30 is the furthest followed by 2.79. 2.73 is further than 2.70.

5. List them in order and check your answer is sensible. If not, go back to Step 2.

   3.75 3.65 3.3 2.79 2.73 2.7
   Work your way down the list. Are they in size order? Yes, so fill in your answer box.

Practice questions

Put these decimals in order. Start with the smallest number.

1. 8.87, 18.28, 7.87, 1.77, 8.7

2. 2.55 km, 55.2 km, 25.52 km, 5.22 km

3. 9.424, 9.442, 9.242, 9.224, 9.99

4. 0.734, 0.73, 0.773, 0.077

Short multiplication

Short multiplication is two- or three-digit numbers multiplied by a single digit number. Your tables will come in useful when doing calculations like these.

What is the product of 482 and 9?

1 Read the question, then read it again.

"product of"... that's multiplication!

2 Picture the numbers. Estimate an answer.

Mmm...
500×10...
Around 5000?

3 Partition the numbers and draw a grid.

×	400	80	2
9			

4 Multiply the numbers.

×	400	80	2
9	3600	720	18

5 Add up the answers.

$3600 + 720 + 18 = 4338$

6 Check your answers. Does it look right? If not, go back to Step 2.

What did I estimate the answer was? About 5000.

7 Check your answer against your estimate. Does it look right? If not, go back to Step 2.

Our answer was fairly close to the estimate. Yes! We were correct.

Practice questions

1 What is 425 multiplied by 6? ☐

2 What is 713 times 4? ☐

3 Multiply 399 and 5. ☐

4 $362 \times 7 =$ ☐

5 $773 \times 9 =$ ☐

6 $639 \times 8 =$ ☐

Short division

Short division is dividing a two- or three-digit number by a single digit. Knowing your tables will help you to do these calculations. Division is the opposite or inverse of multiplication, e.g. $4 \times 5 = 20$, so $20 \div 5 = 4$.

Let's practise!

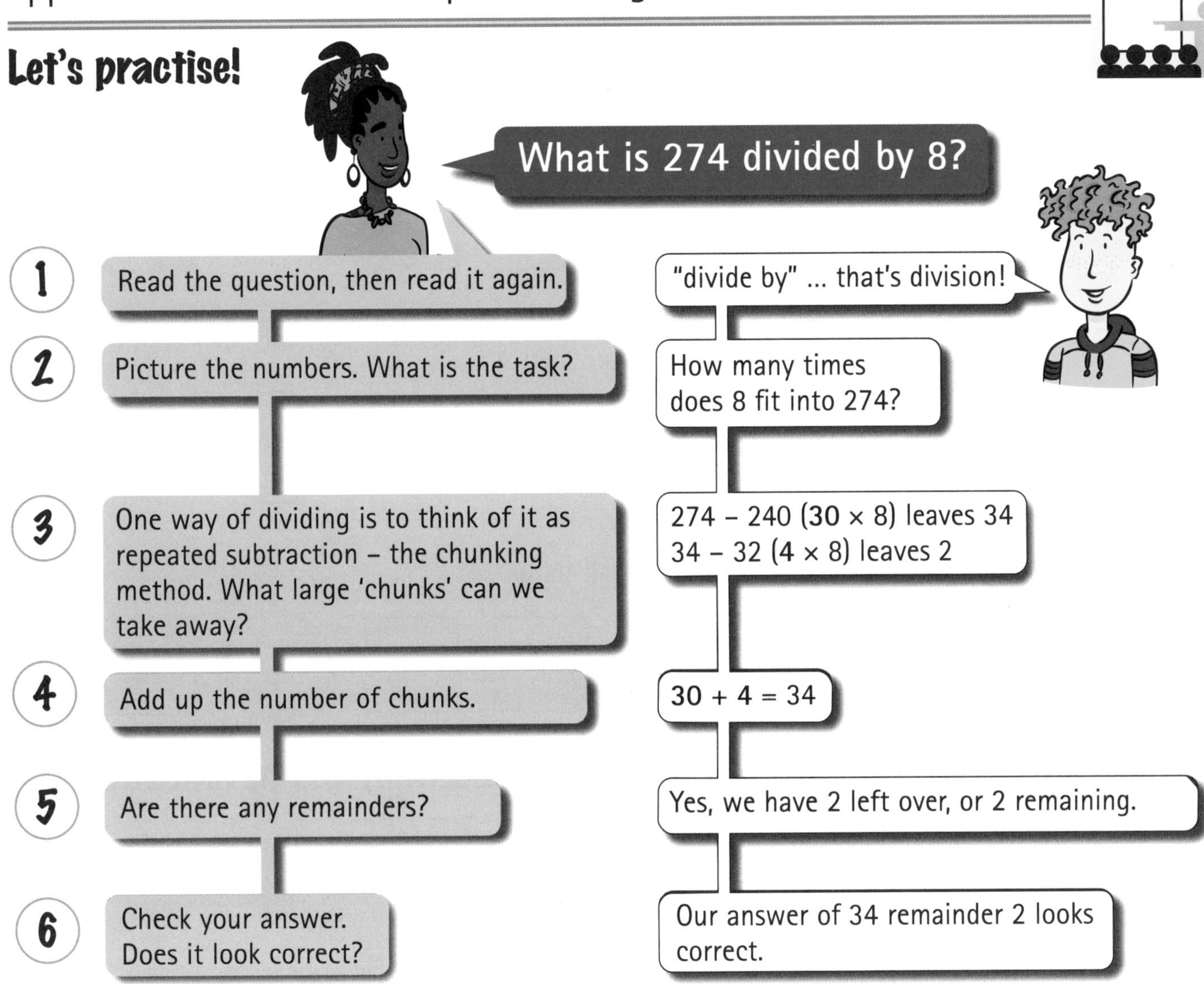

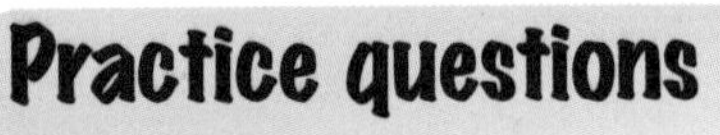

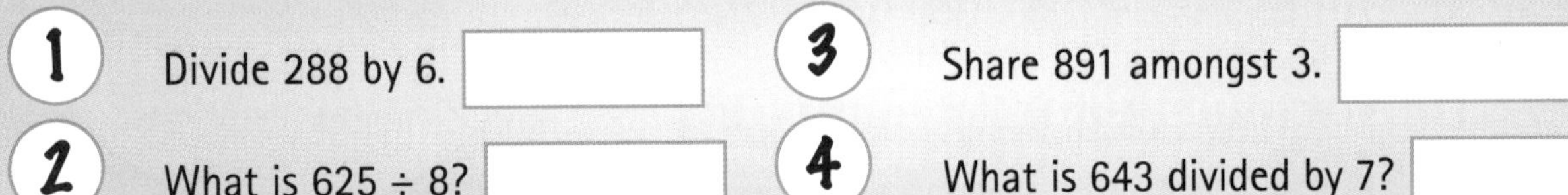

1. Divide 288 by 6.
2. What is $625 \div 8$?
3. Share 891 amongst 3.
4. What is 643 divided by 7?

Recognising proportions of a whole

Important proportions of whole objects

Simple fractions and percentages can be shown in different ways. Have a look at these shapes. Some fractions have been shaded.

These are all halves...

Halves $\frac{1}{2}$ or 50% or 0.5

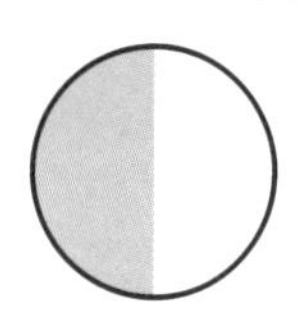 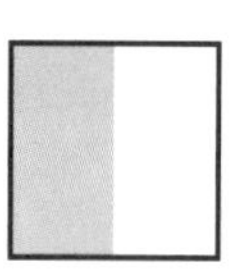 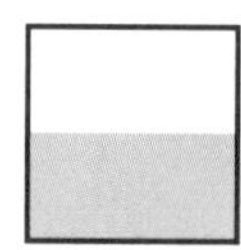 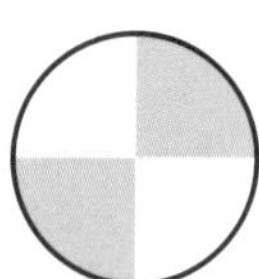 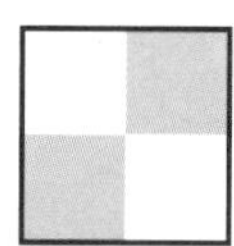

These are all quarters...

Quarters $\frac{1}{4}$ or 25% or 0.25

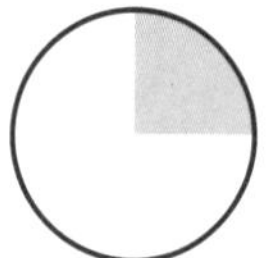   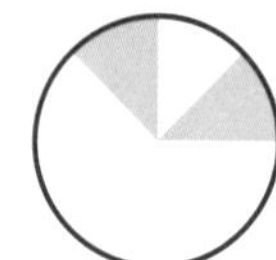 

These are all thirds...

Thirds $\frac{1}{3}$ or 33% (approx.)
or 0.33 (approx.)

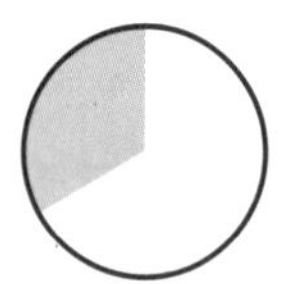 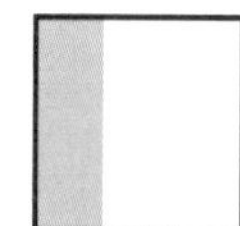 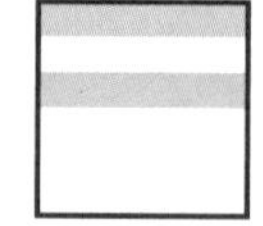 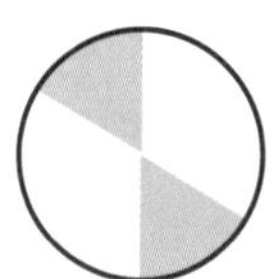 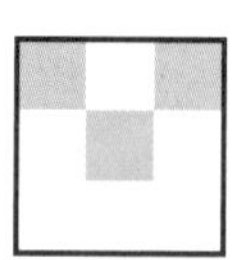

Let's try this simple question. Remember to use what you have learnt above about proportions to help you find the answers.

120 children in Years 5 and 6 were asked what their favourite animal was.

Can you see the shape of 60 out of 120? This is half of the total.

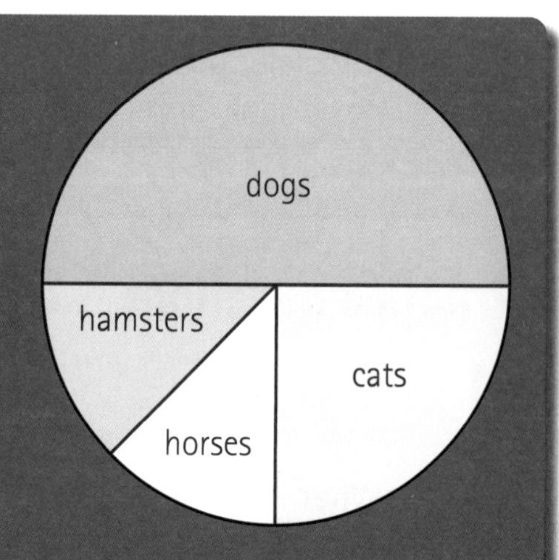

1 Which animal did 60 children choose? ____________

2 How many said the cat was their favourite animal? Can you see the shape of the number of children who chose the cat? It is a quarter.

The answer is $\frac{1}{4}$ of 120 which is ______

More difficult proportions

These shaded proportions are a little harder – but it's easier if you can recognise them straight away! Try to learn them.

Three quarters $\frac{3}{4}$ or 75% or 0.75

These are all three quarters...

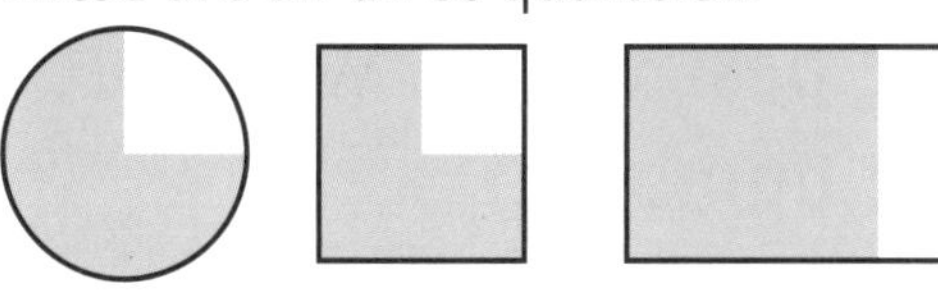

Two thirds $\frac{2}{3}$ or 66% (approx.)
or 0.66 (approx.)

These are all two thirds...

Practice questions

Practise dividing these circles into equal parts. The first slice in each has been done for you.

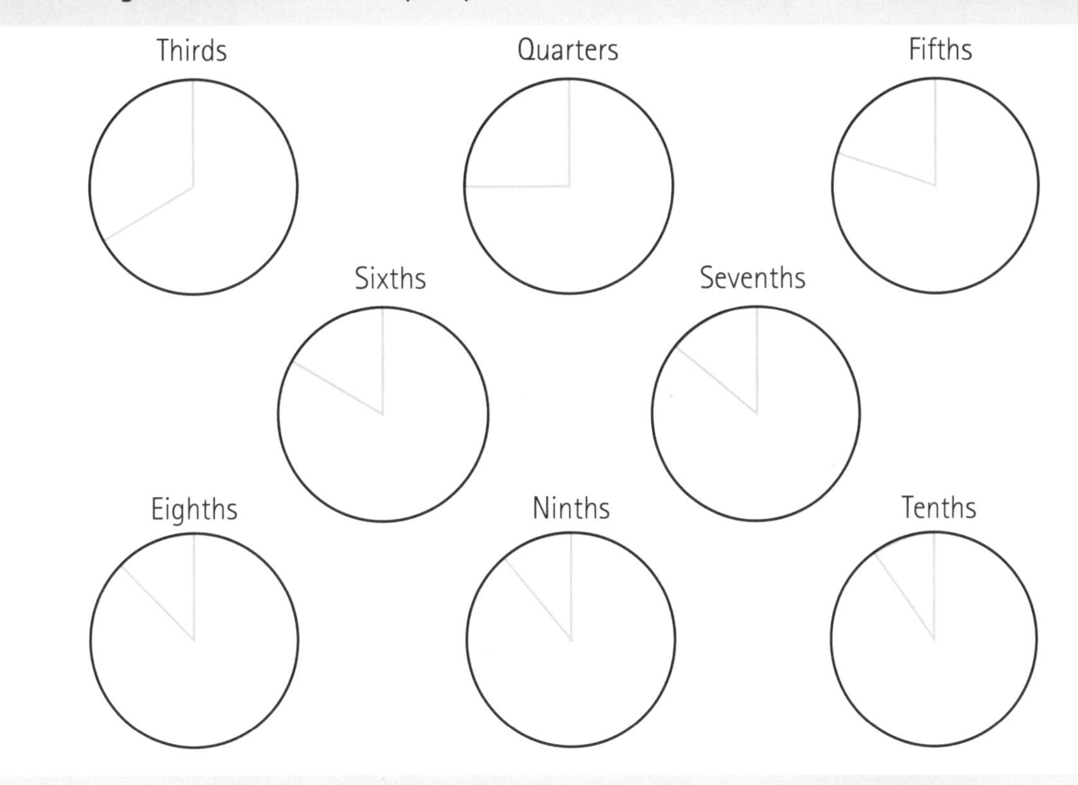

Tip

Try to picture proportions of objects in your head. Look at the cover of this book. How could you divide it up into equal halves or quarters? Visualise dividing different objects into different proportions of their whole.

Number patterns

Number patterns or sequences are lists of numbers that follow a pattern. The best way to work out a sequence is to find the 'difference between' the numbers.

Let's practise!

Fill in the missing numbers and explain the rule in writing.

27, 40, ☐, ☐, 79

1. Read the question then read it again.
   - There are two parts to this question. Don't forget.
2. Picture the numbers.
   - Starting at 27 and going upwards towards 79.
3. Look at the difference between the first two numbers that are next to each other.
   - 27 and 40. The difference is 13.
4. Use the difference you have found and 'test it' on the sequence.
   - 40 + 13 = 53
   - 53 +13 = 66
   - 66 + 13 = 79. It fits!
5. If it fits the sequence, then fill in your answer and explain the rule.
   - Fill in the boxes correctly. 53 66
   - Explain the rule: 'Add 13 each time.'

Practice questions

Try filling in the missing numbers in these sequences. Can you explain each rule?

1. −10, −5, ☐, 5, ☐ ______________________
2. 17, ☐, 51, 68, ☐ ______________________
3. ☐, 118, 95, ☐, ☐ ______________________

We are now going to look at three different types of sequence.

1 Factors

Factors are numbers that divide exactly into other numbers.

The factors of 12 are: 1, 2, 3, 4, 6 and 12

The factors of 10 are: 1, 2, 5 and 10

Practice questions

List the factors of:

1. 32
2. 60
3. 42
4. 80

2 Prime numbers

A prime number is a number that can **only** be divided by ONE and itself.
The first prime numbers are: 2, 3 and 5
If a number doesn't have any other factors then it is called a PRIME NUMBER.

Can you find all the prime numbers up to 100?

3 Multiples

Multiples are numbers made by multiplying two other numbers together.

★ Multiples tips

- If a number is a multiple of 2, the last digit will be even. (20, 22, 24, 26...)
- If a number is a multiple of 3, the sum of its digits can be divided by 3. (57 = 5 + 7 = 12 or 114 = 1 + 1 + 4 = 6)
- If a number is a multiple of 4, the last two digits can be divided by 4. (780 or 436 or 916)
- If a number is a multiple of 5, the last digit is a 0 or a 5. (1055, 260, 475)
- If a number is a multiple of 6, it must be an even number and the sum of its digits must be divisible by 3. (1488 = 1 + 4 + 8 + 8 = 21)
- If a number is a multiple of 7, it is a tricky one and you will just have to work it out the long way. 7 is awkward, it doesn't like rules!
- If a number is a multiple of 8, then half the number can be divided by 4! (528 ÷ 2 = 264 ÷ 4 = 66)
- If a number is a multiple of 9, then the sum of its digits is divisible by 9. (378 = 3 + 7 + 8 = 18)
- If a number is a multiple of 10, then the last digit is 0. (290, 1000, 2020)

Checking your answers

Checking your results should be something you do automatically when you answer a question. It can save you marks in a test and help you to become more accurate with your answers.

Here are five excellent ways you can check the results of your calculations.

Inverse operations

Remember, adding and subtracting are OPPOSITES. Multiplying and dividing are OPPOSITES. We can use this knowledge to check our answers quickly.

EXAMPLE

75 + 95 = 170 Check: 170 − 95 = 75

OR 38 × 6 = 228 Check: 228 ÷ 6 = 38

Practice questions

1. 524 − 67 = ☐ Check: ☐ + 67 = ☐
2. 160 ÷ 4 = ☐ Check: ☐ × 4 = ☐
3. 7884 − 897 = ☐ Check: ☐ + 897 = ☐
4. 2250 ÷ 50 = ☐ Check: ☐ × 50 = ☐

Approximate by rounding

Another way to check your answers is to round the numbers in the question up or down to the nearest 10, 100 or 1000. This will give you a simple sum to do first and give you a rough answer.

EXAMPLE

297 + 805 is about 300 + 800. Easy! 1100

38 × 19 is about 40 × 20. Easy! 800

You can then check your final answer against your rough answer – they should be fairly close. If not, check your rough answer and then your calculation.

Practice questions

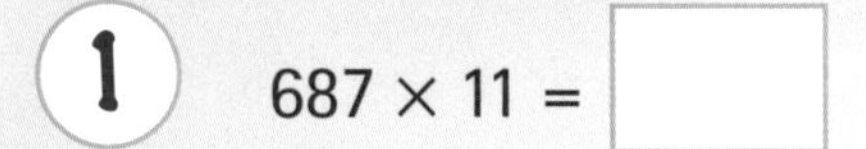

1. 687 × 11 = ☐ Rough answer ______________________
2. 391 − 108 = ☐ Rough answer ______________________
3. 468 ÷ 18 = ☐ Rough answer ______________________

Forwards and backwards

When adding several numbers together, try adding them again but backwards.
It doesn't matter what order you add numbers together, the answer will be the same.

Example
11 + 12 + 13 = 36 or 13 + 12 + 11 = 36

Try this sum, starting from the top of the units column.
Now check by starting at the bottom of the units column and continuing. Were you correct?

$$\begin{array}{r} 374 \\ 536 \\ 28 \\ +\ \ 73 \\ \hline \\ \hline \end{array}$$

Odds and evens

Knowing about odd and even numbers can help with your checking.

ADDITION
- If you add two even numbers, your answer is even.
- If you add two odd numbers, your answer is even.
- If you add one odd and one even number, your answer is odd.

SUBTRACTION
- If you find the difference of two even numbers, your answer is even.
- If you find the difference of two odd numbers, your answer is even.
- If you find the difference of one odd and one even number, your answer is odd.

MULTIPLICATION
- If you multiply two even numbers, your answer is even.
- If you multiply two odd numbers, your answer is odd.
- If you multiply one odd and one even number, your answer is even.

Does your answer 'look right'? (Treat your calculator with care!)

It is always worth taking a couple of seconds to redo a calculation to make sure you have pressed the right buttons.

- Think about the question.
- Look at your answer.
- Does it make sense?

Try this example:

Billy answers the question 435 × 12 on his calculator.
His calculator displays the answer 48 720.

Billy looks at his answer and knows he is wrong.
He redoes the calculation and gets the answer 5220.

Billy used his knowledge of multiplication by 10 and 100 to help him.
Can you work out what Billy did wrong in his first calculation?

Using coordinates

Coordinates are used to identify an exact point on a grid. they are very useful on maps and charts.

Coordinates are written in brackets with a comma in between, e.g. (3, 5).

We always read coordinates ALONG the 'x' axis and up (or down) the 'y' axis.

The 'x' axis is always horizontal and 'y' axis is always vertical.

Have a look at this treasure map.

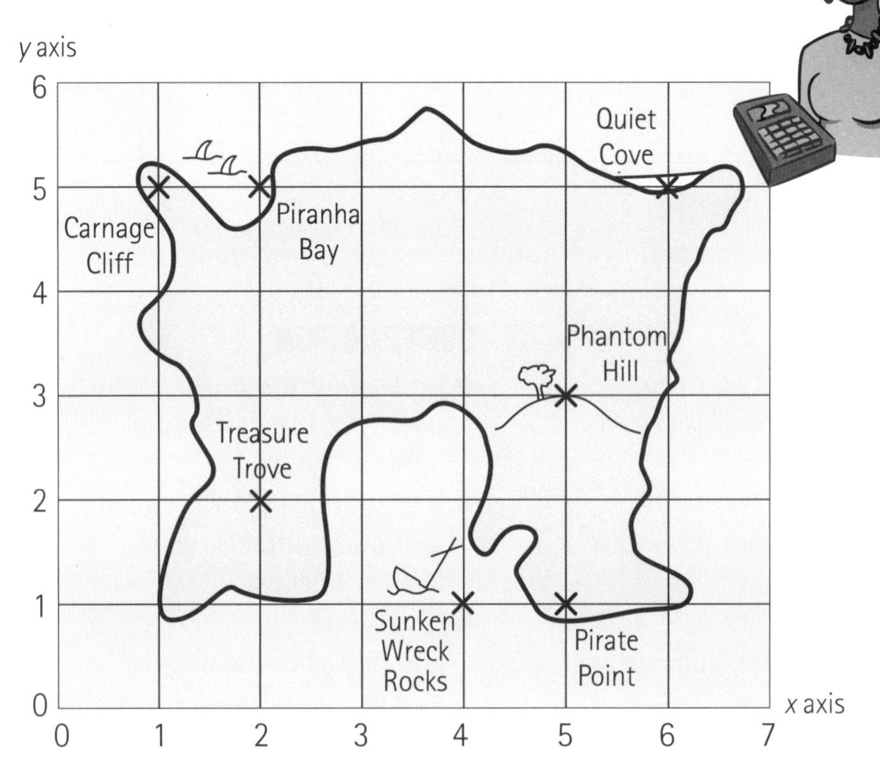

Practice questions

The coordinates of the buried treasure are (2, 2).
Find this on the map.

1 What are the coordinates of: Sunken Wreck Rocks? (_______, _______)
Piranha Bay? (_______, _______)
Quiet Cove? (_______, _______)

2 Where would you be at these points?

(a) (5, 3) ______________________________

(b) (1, 5) ______________________________

(c) (5, 1) ______________________________

Tip 1

Remember 'x' comes before 'y' in the alphabet.

Always go ALONG the corridor THEN UP the stairs.

Tip 2

The point (0, 0) is called the origin.

Finding shapes from a set of coordinates

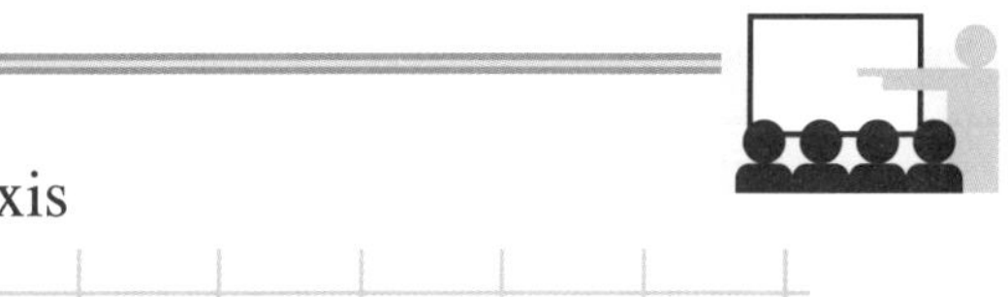

Let's practise!

These points are the coordinates of the vertices of a shape.

(2, 1) (4, 1) (5, 3)
(4, 5) (2, 5) (1, 3)

Plot them on the grid. What is the shape?

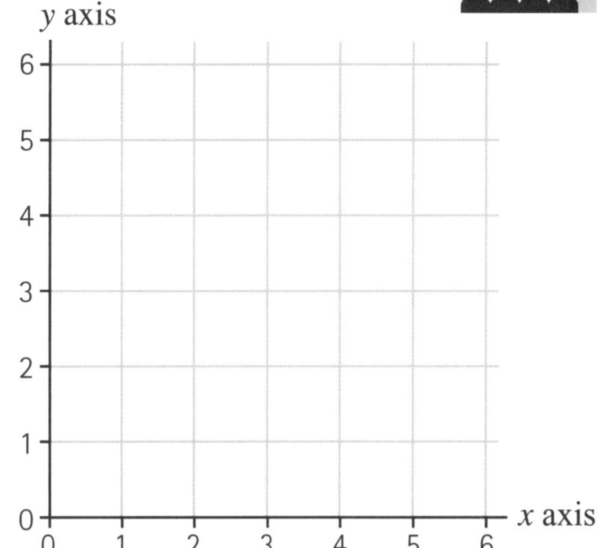

1	Read the question then read it again.	There are words and numbers in this question – read it carefully.
2	Picture the numbers. What do they mean?	The numbers are coordinates.
3	Plot each coordinate in turn.	Go along (*x*) first, then up (*y*). Use your finger first then mark the point with an 'x'.
4	Check each point as you go. Does it look right?	Each time you plot a point, take a look at the shape or pattern that is developing.
5	Join up the points to make the shape.	Lightly draw the shape. Use a ruler and be accurate.
6	Are you happy with the shape? If yes, draw it in. If not, go back to Step 3.	Yes, the shape has 6 sides. It is a regular hexagon.

Practice questions

On the grid above, can you plot the coordinates of:

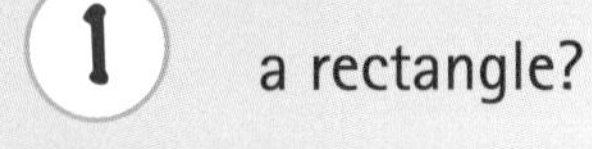

1 a rectangle?

2 a pentagon?

Your shapes can overlap each other.

Write the coordinates here:

Rectangle: (_____, _____) (_____, _____) (_____, _____) (_____, _____)

Pentagon: (_____, _____) (_____, _____) (_____, _____) (_____, _____) (_____, _____)

3D shapes – making models

To get a Level 4 in mathematics you have to be able to imagine what a 3D shape would look like if it was 'unfolded' – that is, when it is a 'net'.

The net of a solid shape is what it looks like when it has been opened out and laid flat.

Imagine unfolding a box of chocolates so that the box is just one piece of card.

Practice questions

Can you link the nets to the 3D shapes? Draw a line to match them up. Try to picture the nets folding themselves up in front of your eyes. Imagination is important in maths you know!

Some shapes, like the cube, have more than one net. Can you see which of these nets would form a cube? Circle them.

Completing a 3D shape

A popular question is to ask you to visualise 3D shapes that have blocks missing.

Let's practise!

What is the least amount of blocks needed to turn this shape into a cuboid?

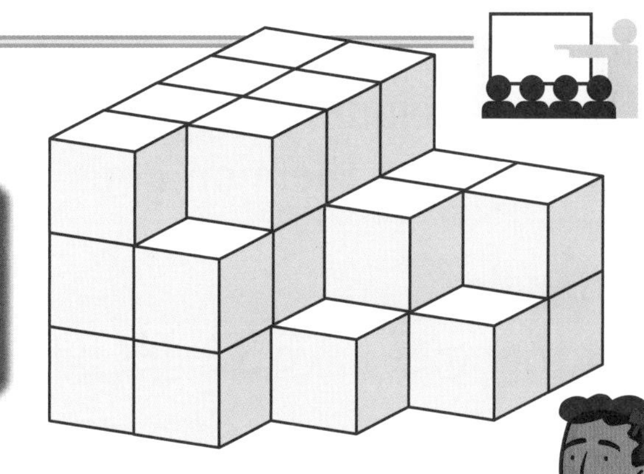

1. Read the question then read it again. — What are you being asked to do?
2. Picture the complete shape in your head. — What would it look like? Think about each block. Don't forget to include the blocks you can't see.
3. Work out the dimensions of the shape. — 'Dimensions' means how many blocks long, wide and high it is. This shape is 4 blocks long, 4 wide and 3 high.
4. Calculate the total number of blocks if the shape was complete. — Right, that's $4 \times 4 \times 3 = 48$. 48 blocks would make up the entire cuboid.
5. Calculate how many blocks are in each layer. — There should be 3 layers of 16 blocks because $3 \times 16 = 48$. Cool!
6. Count how many blocks are missing from each layer to get your answer. — Bottom layer: 3 missing. Middle layer: 5 missing. Top layer: 9 missing. $3 + 5 + 9 = 17$ blocks missing.
7. Does your answer look right? If not, go back to Step 1. — Yes it does. We need 17 blocks to turn this shape into a cuboid.

Practice questions

How many blocks would it take to complete these cuboids?

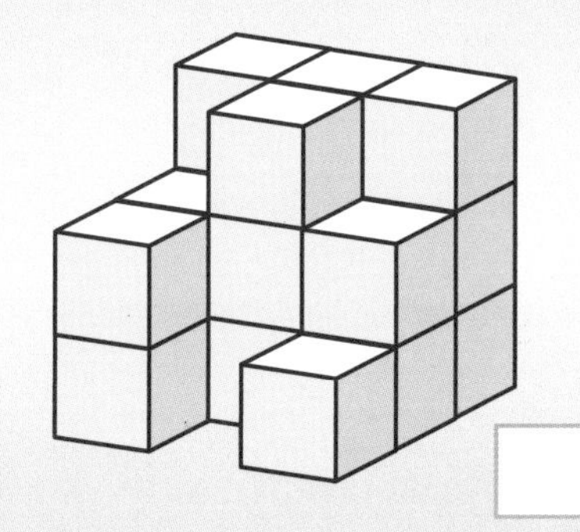

2D shapes

To achieve a Level 4 in mathematics you will need to know all about 2D shapes, including triangles and rectangles. You will also need to know how to draw them on grids.

Triangles

All triangles have 3 sides but there are different types of triangle!

Equilateral

All 3 sides are of equal length.
All 3 angles are equal in size.

Isoceles

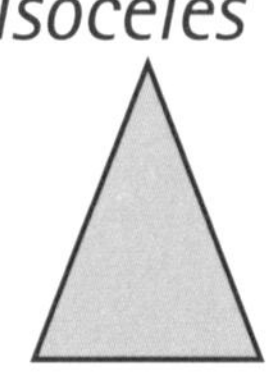

Two sides are equal.
Two angles are equal.

Scalene

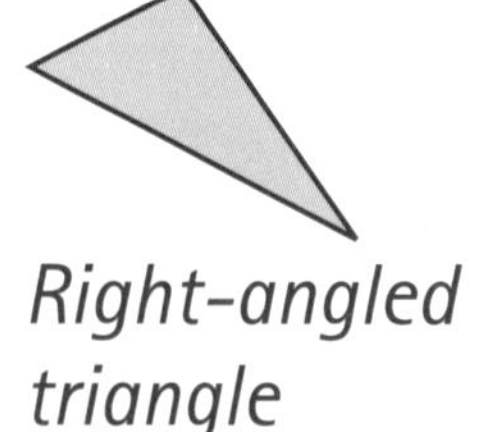

No sides or angles are equal.

Right-angled triangle

One of the angles is a right angle.

Use these grids to draw 3 examples of each triangle.
Make sure the points (or vertices) of each shape are on the dots.

equilateral	isoceles
scalene	right-angled

Tip

Use a sharp pencil and a ruler for this exercise and make sure you have these for your test!

Rectangles

It is important to learn and remember these properties of a rectangle.

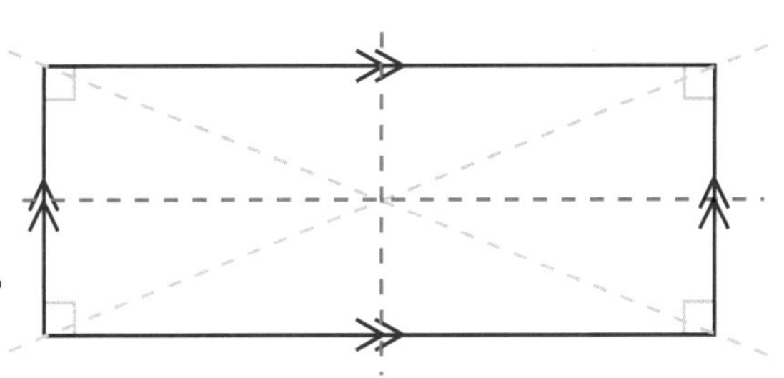

(a) All 4 angles are right angles.

(b) The opposite sides are parallel and equal.

(c) The diagonals bisect each other (blue lines).

(d) There are 2 lines of symmetry (red lines).

KEY FACTS

Parallel = lines that never meet and are always the same distance from one another. This symbol shows when two lines are parallel ≪.
Bisect = when the lines cross they divide the rectangle into equal parts.
Square = a rectangle with four equal sides!

Use this grid to draw 5 rectangles of different sizes.

Reflections of simple shapes in a mirror line

You should be familiar with reflecting simple shapes – see page 13.
To achieve a Level 4 you need to be able to reflect shapes where either the shape or the mirror line, or both, are at an angle.

For example:

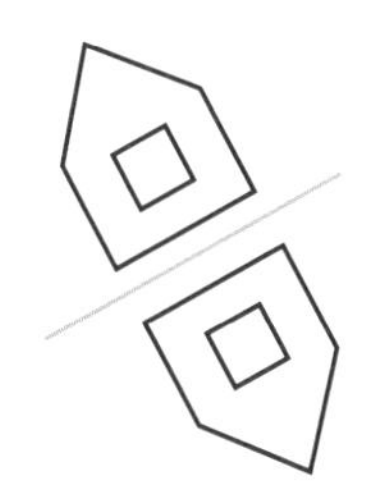

Now try these:

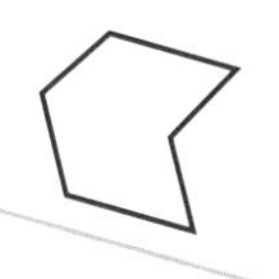

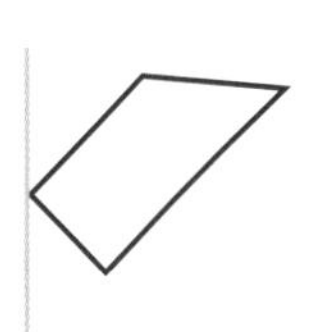

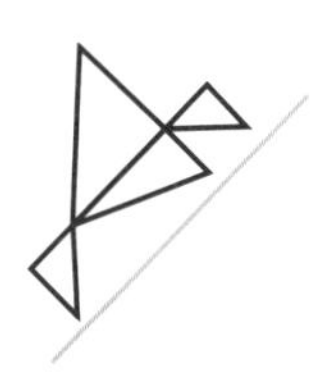

Tip

When sketching a reflection, picture what the reflection would look like before you draw it.

Finding the perimeters of simple shapes

The perimeter of a shape is the distance all the way around its edge. This is very easy to work out as long as you remember to follow a step-by-step guide.

Let's practise!

What is the perimeter of this shape?

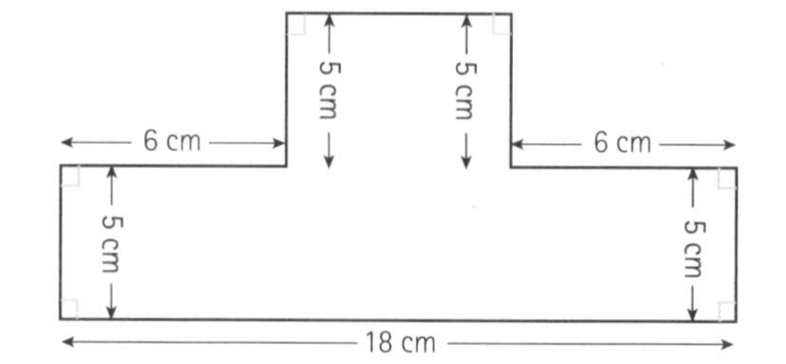

1. Read the question then read it again.
   "Perimeter of". We are being asked to measure the distance around the shape.
2. Choose a side to start from.
   Put a line through it with your pencil. This is the clever part. It helps you to remember where you started.
3. Add up all the lengths that are given in the question.
   5 cm + 6 cm + 5 cm + 18 cm + 5 cm + 6 cm + 5 cm = 50 cm
4. Now work out the length of the side you haven't been given.
   This is the important part. The right angles show you that the distance along the top of the shape must be the same as the distance along the bottom. **Both must be 18 cm.** The **missing** side must be 6 cm because 6 cm + 6 cm + 6 cm = 18 cm.
5. Add the missing length to the total of the lengths you have been given.
   50 cm + 6 cm = 56 cm
6. Does your answer look sensible? If so put it in the box.
   The perimeter of the shape is 56 cm.

Tip

In this type of question, don't try to measure missing sides with a ruler. The reason they are missing is to test to see if you can work them out from the given lengths.

A perimeter fence goes ALL THE WAY AROUND a building like a prison or a military base.

Finding areas of shapes by counting

To achieve a Level 4 you will need to find the area of a tricky shape that has been drawn onto squared paper.

KEY FACTS

The area of a shape is the amount of the surface it covers.

Make sure the units you write are always squared, e.g. cm^2 or m^2.

Let's practise!

Each square is 1 square centimetre. What area is shaded?

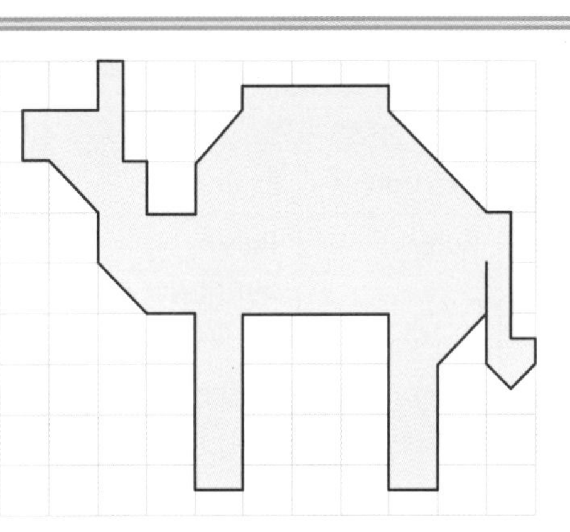

1. Read the question then read it again.
   It is the shaded squares we have to count.
2. Start by counting the whole squares, ticking them off as each is counted.
   Start at the top row and move your finger along to the end counting any **whole** squares. Repeat on the next row. Jot down the total: **31 squares.**
3. Now count the $\frac{3}{4}$ shaded squares.
   OK, start from the top row and work downwards. Jot down the total: **one $\frac{3}{4}$ square.**

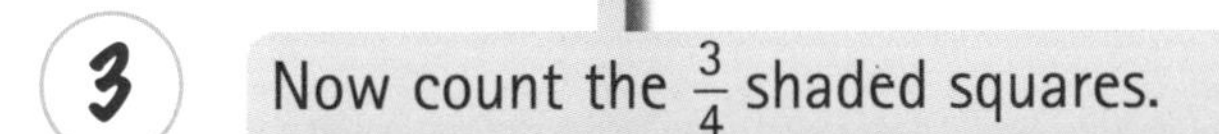

4. Now count the $\frac{1}{2}$ shaded squares.
   There are **sixteen $\frac{1}{2}$ squares.**
5. Now count the $\frac{1}{4}$ shaded squares.
   Back to the top again. Work carefully – **there is one $\frac{1}{4}$ square.**
6. Now add together all the fractions.
   One times $\frac{3}{4} = \frac{3}{4}$; sixteen halves = 8; one quarter $= \frac{1}{4}$. That makes 9 whole squares.
7. Add the units and square your answer. Does it look sensible?
   31 whole squares + 9 whole squares = 40 cm^2.

Measures

To achieve a Level 4 in mathematics it is important that you know the following things about measures.

(a) Which units of measure to use when measuring length, mass and capacity.

(b) Which instruments to use when measuring length, mass and capacity.

(c) How to read those instruments.

Use the table on this page to learn about the first two!

	Length of			Mass (weight of)			Capacity of		
	Unit	Instrument	Example	Unit	Instrument	Example	Unit	Instrument	Example
Small	mm	Ruler	Raisin Sunflower seed	g	Scales	Newspaper Chocolate bar	ml	Teaspoon	Food colouring for cakes
Medium	cm	Ruler Metre rule	DVD case Your foot	kg	Bathroom scales	A bag of cement Yourself	cl	Measuring jug	Can of cola Glass of milk
Large	m km	Tape measure Metre wheel Tachometer	Distance you can ride a bike	kg tonne	Large scales Weigh bridge	Rhinoceros Tractor	l	Container of of known capacity	Capacity of aquarium Swimming pool

Here are some questions about the table.

1. Name something you would measure in centimetres.

2. Name something you would measure in centilitres.

3. What instrument would you use to measure the weight of the newspaper?

4. What instrument would you use to measure the length of a sunflower seed?

5. Think of two different things you could measure in:

(a) kg ______ and ______

(b) l ______ and ______

(c) km ______ and ______

Use the table as a guide. Think of some other objects or distances. Where would you 'place' them on the table?

Reading scales

At Level 4 it is important that you understand how to read instruments of measurement, most of which use scales. The scale will tell you how many of the units of measurement the instrument has measured. The scale might be a dial on a set of scales, lines on the side of a jug or ruler, or decimal numbers in a display.

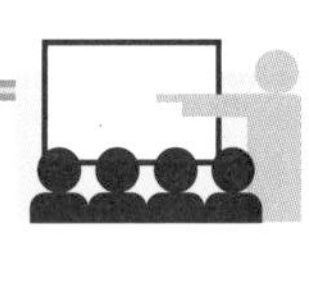

Let's practise!

ml 500
400
300
200
100

350 ml more water is poured into the cylinder. Mark the new level.

1	Read the question then read it again.	We are dealing with measures so we need to be accurate.
2	Picture the numbers.	"350 ml more"
3	Check the unit. What is it: g, l, km?	The measuring cylinder is marked in ml – that's millilitres.
4	If the indicator is on a numbered level, read off that level.	It is between 100 ml and 200 ml.
5	If the indicator is between numbers, then work out what each mark is worth and count forwards or backwards.	OK. The scale goes up by 10 ml each time.
6	Calculate the sum. Mark on the measurement.	140 ml plus 350 more = 490 ml.

Grouping data

Frequency charts might have grouped data. This makes the data easier to handle.

Here is a chart showing the number of questions answered correctly by 16 children on a school quiz with 30 questions. We wanted to find out what the most common mark was.

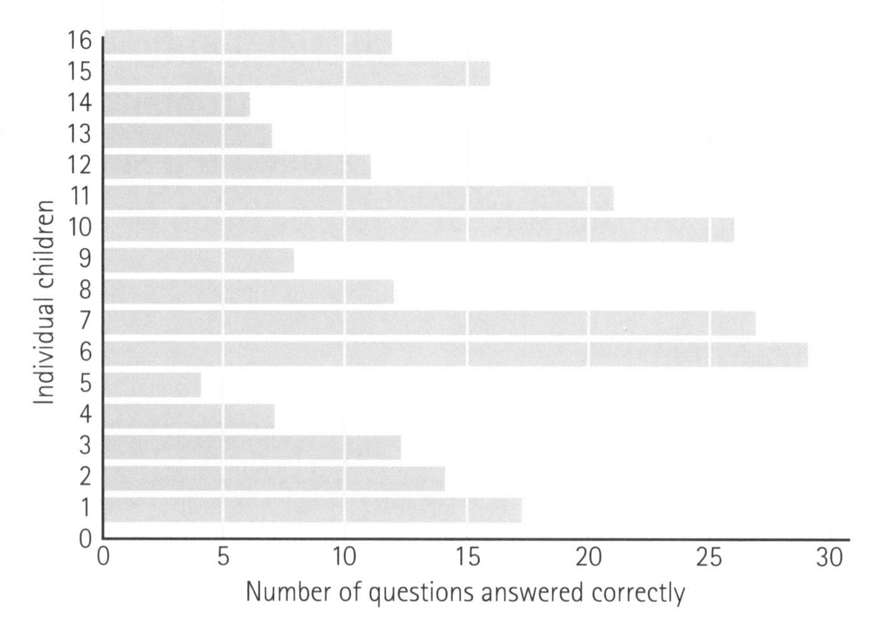

This looks quite complicated! We can make it easier if we group the scores and then compare them. Look at the new chart and answer the questions below.

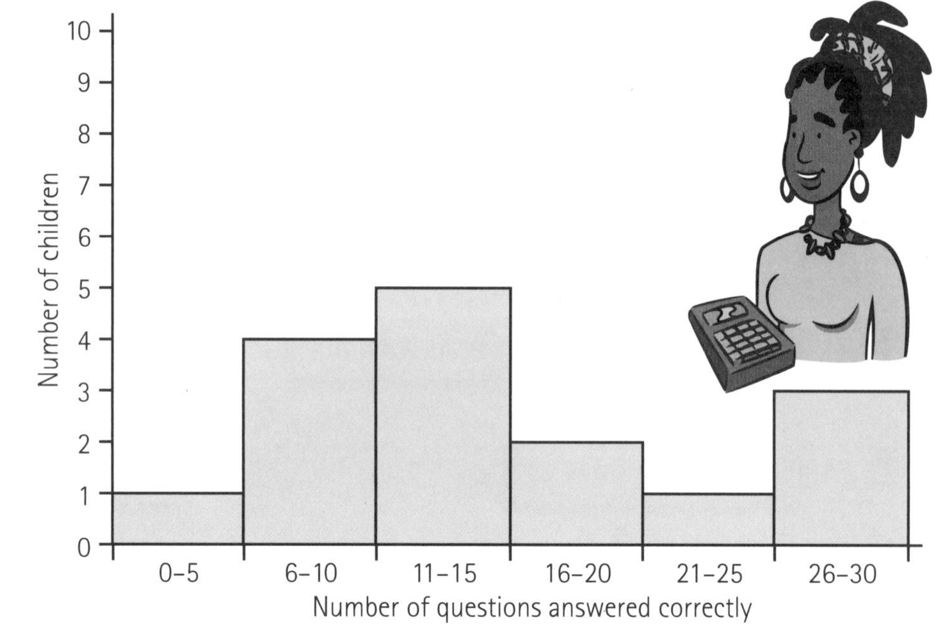

Questions

1. How many children scored between 16 and 20 marks?
2. How many children scored more than 15 marks?
3. What was the second most common range of scores in the quiz?
4. How many children scored fewer than 21 marks?
5. Look at both of the charts. Did anyone get all the questions right?

Let's practise!

A week later some children answered the same questions again. Their scores had improved! Here are the results. Can you draw a bar chart and group the data? What was the most common score?

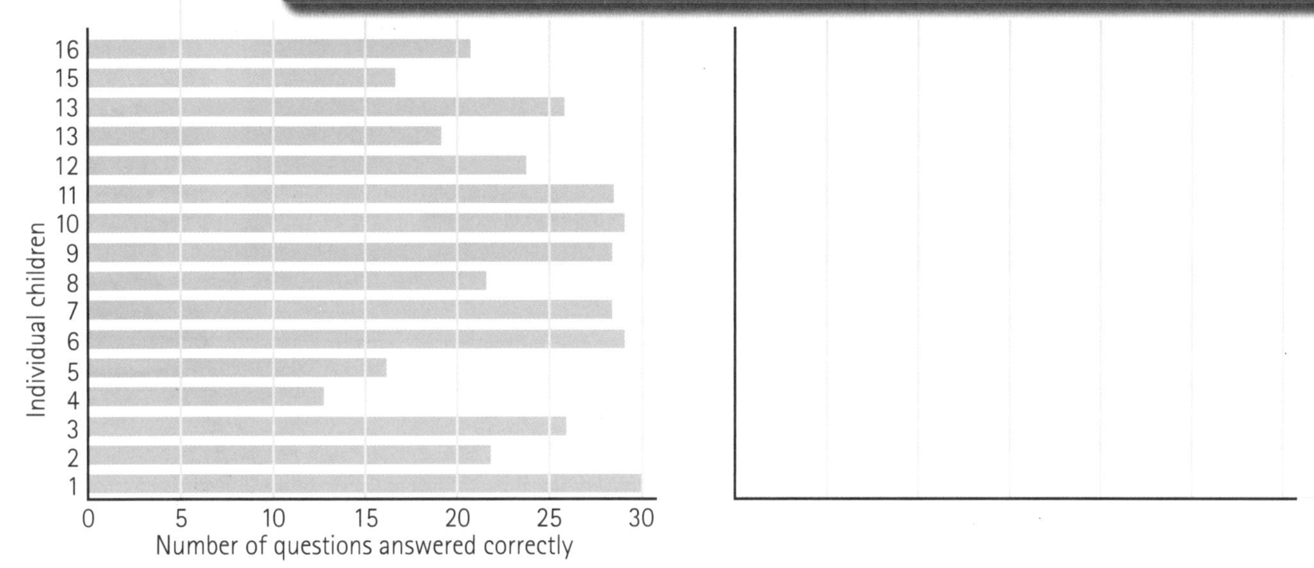

1. Read the question then read it again.

... draw the chart and find the most common score ...

2. Group the data in equal amounts. Mark on your axis.

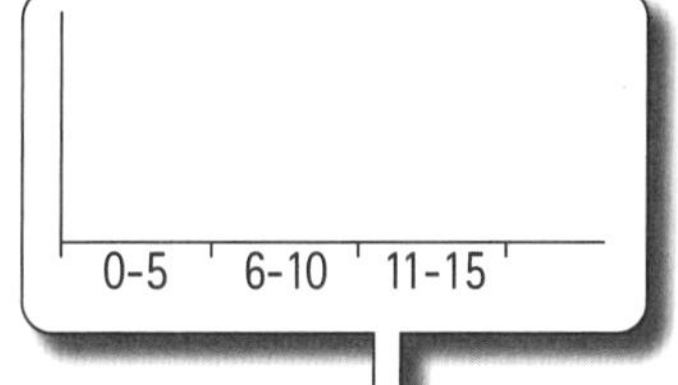

3. Tally the number for each group of data.

OK. The first group is 0-5. How many children scored 0-5? None, now the next group. None again. Now the 11-15 group. Ah! One. Next the 16-20 group... 3. Next the 21-25 group... 4. Finally the 26-30 group... 8.

4. Draw in the bars.

The most common score is now between 26 and 30.

5. Check your results. Do they look sensible?

Yes, the children scored much higher. This looks right.

Tip

Think clearly. Work step-by-step.

When handling data, a rough piece of paper can be useful to make notes or tally information.

Finding the range

To achieve a Level 4 you will need to find the range of a series of data.

Let's practise!

This is the price of the same cookery book in four different shops:

£8.99 £14.49 £10.98 £10

What is the range of these prices?

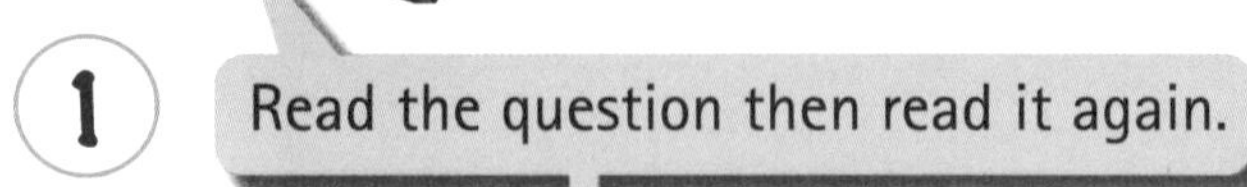

1. Read the question then read it again.

2. Think about the question. — The range is the difference between the **lowest** and **highest** value.

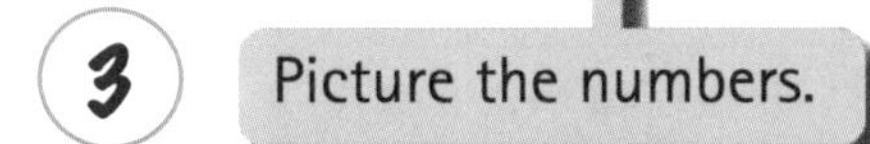

3. Picture the numbers. — Put them in order, lowest first: £8.99, £10, £10.98 and £14.49.
4. Study the numbers. — The most expensive is £14.49. The cheapest is £8.99. What is the difference between these costs?
5. Calculate your answer. — £14.49 – £8.99 = £5.50
6. If your answer looks sensible, write it in the box. — If not, go back to Step 3 and try again.

Practice question

Rising Stars Bookshop sells lots of books. What was the range of books sold for the second half of 2002?

2002

July	16 700	August	23 414	September	11 103
October	25 777	November	28 993	December	30 444

Tip

Scan the list and mark the lowest number.

Tip

Check through the list to see if it really is the lowest. Repeat for the highest number.

Finding the mode

Your test might also contain questions on mode.

Let's practise!

These are the ages of the Bright Stars football team.

18 22 23 29 22 18 29 23 22 23 22

What is the mode of these ages?

1. Read the question then read it again.
2. Think about the question. — The mode is another name for the most common value.
3. Picture the numbers. — Make sets of the same number.

18	22	23	29
18	22	23	29
	22	23	
	22		

4. Double-check. — Make sure you haven't missed any numbers.
5. Decide on your answer. — 22 occurs most often. **22 is the mode.**
6. If your answer looks sensible, write it in the box. — If not, go back to Step 3 and try again.

Practice question

The children in Class 4 have different numbers of brothers and sisters. What is the mode of the number of siblings?

2 4 1 0 0 2 1 3 2 3 4

Remember:

Mode is the Most Common Value

Modal means Mode

Always write out the numbers again and sort them.

Tick off each number so you know you haven't missed any of them. **This is IMPORTANT!**

Line graphs

A graph with **time** on the *x* **axis** (horizontal) and **numbers** on the *y* **axis** (vertical) is often shown with a line.

Sometimes the graph will show a set of points, joined together by a line. This shows how something is changing over the course of time.

Here is a line graph showing the monthly sales of 'Dudestars™' surfboards over the course of a year.

The line in between the points shows a trend or how the sales are changing. It doesn't have any value – only the points themselves have a value.

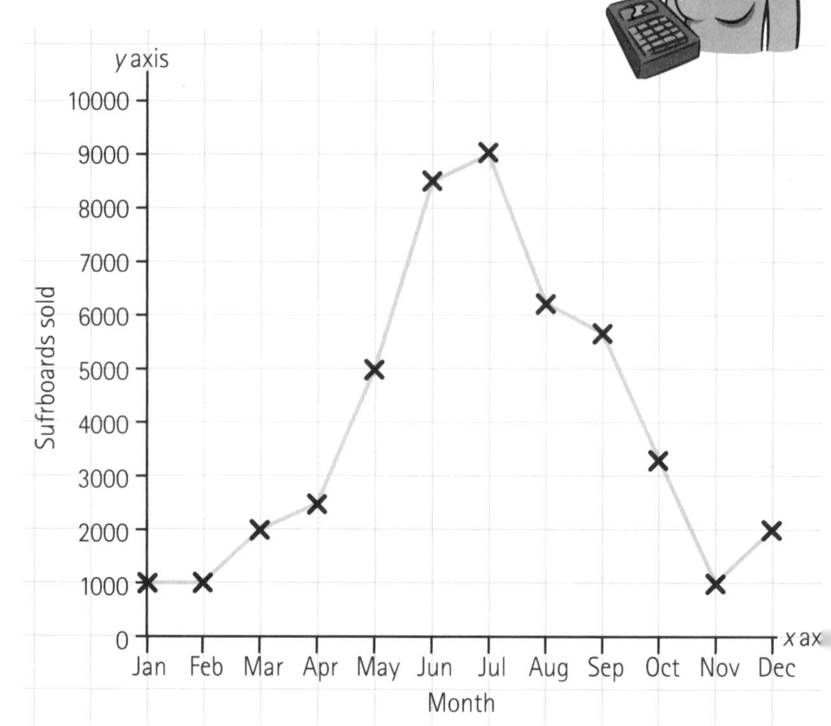

Try answering these questions.

1. Which was the second most successful month? ____________________

   How many surfboards were sold in that month? ____________________

2. Between which two months did the sales of 'Dudestars™' first start to go up?

   ____________________ and ____________________

3. Between which two months did the sales of 'Dudestars™' first start to fall?

   ____________________ and ____________________

4. In which months were more than 6000 surfboards sold? ____________________ and

   ____________________ and ____________________

5. Why do you think there was a rise between November and December? ____________________

Tip

When reading graphs, go UP from the *x* axis first to meet the line, and then go ACROSS to the *y* axis to read the value.

Chaucer School's foorball team kept a record of their league position each month throughout the season. Can you display this information on a line graph?

Month	Aug	Sept	Oct	Nov	Dec	Jan	Feb	Mar	Apr	May
Position	12th	8th	7th	5th	2nd	2nd	1st	3rd	3rd	4th

1. Read the question then read it again. — You need to draw a line graph.
2. Decide which information fits on each axis. — League position (numbers) on the *y* axis and month (time) on the *x* axis.
3. Decide on a scale. — *We need a scale for the league position. The highest is 1st and the lowest is 12th. The range 1-12 seems the most sensible.
4. Plot the points. — This must be accurate. Starting on the *x* axis with August work along to May.
5. Join the points to show the trend. — Does it look like the results in the table?

*You might like to reverse the *y* axis, starting with 12th at the bottom and working up to 1st at the top. This will make it easier to understand when you read it again.

Put the information on the graph using the flow chart to help you. Then answer the questions below.

1. How many months were the team in the top three positions? ________________
2. Between which two months did their league position improve the most? ________________ and ________________
3. How many places did the team drop from February to the end of the season? ____________

★ Tip

Always use a sharp pencil when plotting points – it helps you to be more accurate.

Using simple formulae

A formula is a way of explaining a rule. To achieve a Level 4 you need to be able to explain a given rule in writing.

Let's practise!

Explain how to find the number of months in any number of years.

1. Read the question then read it again.
   It is all words. You have to work out any numbers involved.
2. Picture the numbers and the words.
   The key word here is 'explain'. You also need to show that there are 12 months in a year.
3. Talk through the rule in your head.
   To find the number of months in any number of years, you must multiply the number of years by 12...
4. Test your rule. Does it work? If not, go back to Step 1.
   Make your test simple to avoid mistakes, e.g. 4 years = 4 × 12 = 48 months.
5. Write your rule as simply as possible.
   'The number of months in any number of years = the number of years multiplied by 12.'
6. Check your answer. Does it make sense?
   Read it through to yourself. Does your formula work?

★ Tip 1

Rehearse your sentences in your head before you write them.
When you have written them, read them back to yourself. Have you thought clearly?
Have you said what you wanted to say?

The '=' sign means 'the same as'

e.g. $2 + 2 = 4$ — 2 + 2 is the same as 4

$10 - 5 = 8 - 3$ — 10 − 5 is the same as 8 − 3

A simple formula is often used to find out the total cost of items bought. In words this formula can be written:

"The total cost is the cost for one item multiplied by the number of those items bought."

In letter formulae this could be written as: $T = P \times N$

T = total cost   P = cost of each item   N = number of items bought

Practice questions

Use the $T = P \times N$ formula to work out these questions.

1. What is the value of T if $N = 2$ and $P = £4.50$?
2. What is the value of N if $T = £20$ and $P = £4$?
3. What is the value of P if $T = £24$ and $N = 6$?

Example question

Andrea and Jamie are playing a number game. Jamie gives Andrea a number, which she changes using a rule:

"I take Jamie's number and multiply it by 7, then subtract 2."

Write a formula to show the process Andrea goes through to get to her answer.

Use J for Jamie's number and A for Andrea's answer.

$A = (J \times 7) - 2$

Practice questions

Now Andrea changes the rule:

"I take Jamie's number and multiply it by 9 then add 3."

Write a formula to show the process Andrea goes through to get to her answer. Use J for Jamie's number and A for Andrea's answer.

A =

Tip

If a number and a letter are next to each other, e.g. 4N, it means they are multiplied. Why is the $\times$ (multiply) symbol left out? Because it could get confused with the letter x!

Using and applying mathematics

Introduction

The reason for learning all the different mathematical skills (multiplying, dividing, measuring, estimating and so on) is so you can use them to solve mathematical problems.

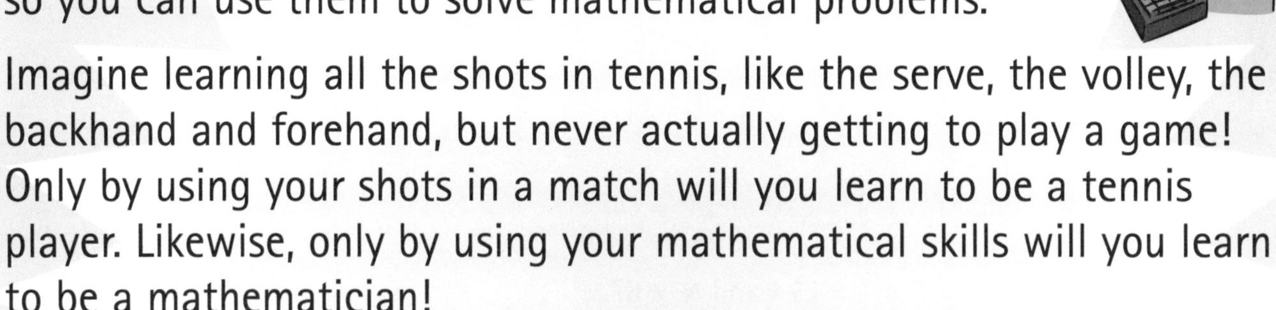

Imagine learning all the shots in tennis, like the serve, the volley, the backhand and forehand, but never actually getting to play a game! Only by using your shots in a match will you learn to be a tennis player. Likewise, only by using your mathematical skills will you learn to be a mathematician!

The flow chart opposite is designed to guide you when tackling a maths problem. It will help organise your thinking, but it won't tell you the answer – that's for you to work out for yourself.

The next few pages contain problems for you to solve. Work through the examples first and then have a go at the practice questions using the flow chart approach.

Good luck!

Problem solving

NUMBER

These questions are all about your number skills. You must use them in the right way though!

MEASURES

These questions are all about real situations: going on a journey, the amount of milk a family drinks in a week and so on.

SHAPE AND SPACE

These questions all require you to use your knowledge about shapes, both 2D and 3D.

HANDLING DATA

These questions often ask you to find out information from a table or chart. They will also ask you to explain how you found out the answer!

The Problem Solving Flow Chart

1. Read the question then read it again.
   Read through the question slowly. Twice. Let the words and numbers 'sink in'.

2. Picture the words and numbers. What do they mean?
   What does this problem mean to you? You could draw a picture or diagram to help you. You could write it in your own words.

3. Highlight key words and phrases.
   Look for mathematical phrases like 'find the difference between', and 'what is the product of'. Work out what is important information and what isn't.

4. Can you estimate an answer?
   This will depend on the question. Estimate using the information you have. Don't guess wildly.

5. What calculations do you need to do?
   Work out what needs to be added, subtracted, multiplied and divided. Sometimes you may need to perform more than one function. Write the calculations down but don't do them yet.

6. What is the answer to your calculations? Show how you got your answer.
   Now calculate if you need to. Estimate first. Write down your method – it shows how well you are thinking. Check your answer.

7. What is the answer to the original problem? Write it in full sentences.
   Does your answer match what you have been asked to do? Don't just give one word or number answers (e.g. 12). Write it in a clear sentence (e.g. The number that Sofie was thinking of was 12.)

8. Is your answer a sensible one?
   Does your answer make sense? Is it realistic? If the problem is a real-life problem, have you got a real-life answer?

★ Tips

- ★ Remember your 'checking the answer' skills.
- ★ Think clearly and write clearly.
- ★ Present your work so it shows what you have done.
- ★ Work step-by-step.
- ★ Make a problem easier (e.g. Find 24 lots of 6. Try finding 4 lots first then 20 lots.)
- ★ Take a reasonable guess at what you think might happen.
- ★ Think HOW you are working. Change your method if something isn't working.
- ★ Look for patterns in your maths.

Solving number problems

Let's try a simple number problem.

The numbers in row 2 of this triangle of snooker balls have been found from the two numbers directly above them using a rule. Fill in the missing numbers and write the rule.

Row 1 84 72 88 44
Row 2 78 80 66
Row 3
Row 4

Rule:

1	Read the question then read it again.	There are two things to do to complete this question – "find the missing numbers" and "write the rule".
2	Picture the words and numbers. What do they mean?	How are these numbers 'linked'? When we have worked it out, we need to *explain* how.
3	Highlight key words and phrases.	"numbers in row 2", "found from the two numbers directly above".
4	Can you estimate an answer?	No, because the answer is not immediately obvious.
5	What calculations do you need to do?	Work step-by-step. Start with 84 and 72. What do we have to do to get 78… Add? Subtract?
6	What is the answer to your calculations? Show how you got your answer.	$84 + 72 = 156$ and $84 - 72 = 12$… Look at our answers. Can we see any 'link' with 78? Yes! 78 is half of 156 or double 78 is 156. Have we found the rule?
7	What is the answer to the original problem? Write it in full sentences.	The rule is add the two numbers together and divide the total by two. We can also fill in the missing numbers. $(78 + 80) \div 2 = 79$; $(80 + 66) \div 2 = 73$; $(79 + 73) \div 2 = 76$
8	Is your answer a sensible one?	Yes, we've applied our rule throughout the triangle and it works!

Practice questions

Use the flow chart to help you to answer this number problem 'story'. Show your method for each calculation you do.

Crime boss 'Eadcase 'Arry suspects his two top henchmen, Baz and Gaz, of being thieves. As if! 'Eadcase decides to find out by setting them a little test – trial by shopping! If they're so much as a penny short, he'll show them how he got his nickname… 'Eadcase tells Baz and Gaz that their hideout is looking a bit scruffy and that it needs a good makeover. He gives them £250 each to spend in ODEA – the home improvement store. However, 'Eadcase wants all receipts and any change that's left over. Any thieving and he'll know about it! This is how Baz and Gaz spend the money…

1 Baz gave the cashier £250 and got £88.01 change. How much were the candles?

Baz's Receipt
Lounge furnishings
Light oak coffee table £95
Sheepskin rug £32
Soft-light lamp £16.99
Candles

Show your method.

2 Gaz gave the cashier £250 and got £38.01 change. How much was the fondue set?

Gaz's Receipt
Kitchen additions
Juicer £95
Seven-piece saucepan set £62
Butchers' block £29.99
Fondue set

Show your method.

3 Baz and Gaz pay £25 to have the goods delivered and £17.60 for a taxi back to the hideout. They give 'Eadcase 'Arry his £83.32 change and receipts… Explain how this story ends, giving your reasons!

Solving measures problems

Let's try a simple measures problem.

Here is a list of ingredients for banana mousse.
It feeds 4 people.

1.2 kg of bananas — 6 eggs
300 ml milk — 4 tablespoons caster sugar

Gordon wants to prepare banana mousse for 6 people.
Can you change the amount of each ingredient so he makes enough mousse? **Show your method:**

1. Read the question then read it again.
   - Change the amounts of four ingredients...
2. Picture the words and numbers. What do they mean?
   - We could draw each item. 4×300 g = 1.2 kg.
3. Highlight key words and phrases.
   - Change the amounts from 4 to 6. Ah! That's an increase of 'half as much again' or 50%.
4. Can you estimate an answer?
   - We can easily work out the number of eggs and the amount of sugar. Gordon now needs 6 eggs plus half as many again, so that's 9 eggs, and 6 tablespoons $(4 + 2)$ of sugar. We can estimate an answer of 1.5 kg of bananas and 500 ml of milk.
5. What calculations do you need to do?
   - (50% of 1.2 kg) + 1.2 kg
   - (50% of 300 ml) + 300 ml.
6. What is the answer to your calculations. Show how you got your answer.
   - 50% of 1.2 kg = 600 g.
   - 1200 g + 600 g = 1800 g or 1.8 kg.
   - 50% of 300 ml = 150 ml
   - 300 ml + 150 ml = 450 ml
7. What is the answer to the original problem? Write it in full sentences.
   - Check answers against our estimate. Gordon would need 1.8 kg of bananas, 450 ml of milk, 9 eggs and 6 tablespoons of sugar.
8. Is your answer a sensible one?
   - Yes, these look sensible amounts for 6 banana mousse!

Practice questions

Use the flow chart to help you answer these questions about measure.
The fun-fair is in town!

1. Mystery Rose has made 400 litres of her special hedgerow punch for the visitors to sample. One cup of punch is 250 ml. How many cups of punch can Mystery Rose sell?

Show your method.

2. The Grand Canyon rollercoaster is 328 m long. If a ride on the rollercoaster is 6 laps long, how far does the rider travel? Give your answer in metres, and then kilometres.

Show your method.

3. The strongman Billy Biceps is demonstrating his great strength. He puts 4 children into a bathtub and lifts them all above his head! The children weigh 46.5 kg, 39 kg, 52.8 kg and 33.2 kg. The bathtub weighs 30 kg. How much does Billy Biceps manage to lift altogether.

Show your method.

4. The Tunnel of Love water ride has sprung 4 leaks. The ride contains 10 000 litres of water. Each leak loses 482 litres. How much water is left for the ride to operate?

Show your method.

5. A customer on the ferris wheel travels 1344 m during the course of the ride. One revolution of the wheel is 56 m. How many times does the wheel revolve for one ride?

Show your method.

6. The Tubbs, a hungry family of 6, eat toffee apples and popcorn during their visit to the fair. Each of the Tubbs eats 350 g of toffee apples and 475 g of popcorn. How many kilograms of food do the family Tubbs consume?

Show your method.

Solving shape and space problems

Let's try a simple shape and space problem.

How many rectangles can you see in this shape?

Show your method:

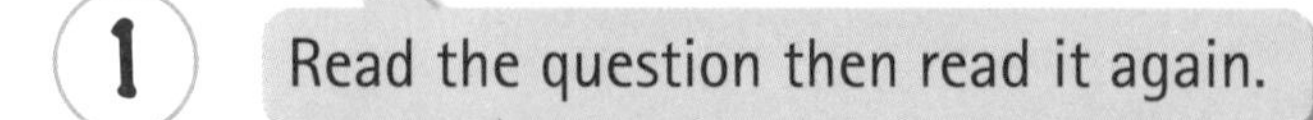

1. Read the question then read it again.

Study the words. Study the shape. Think past 'the obvious'.

2. Picture the words and numbers. What do they mean?

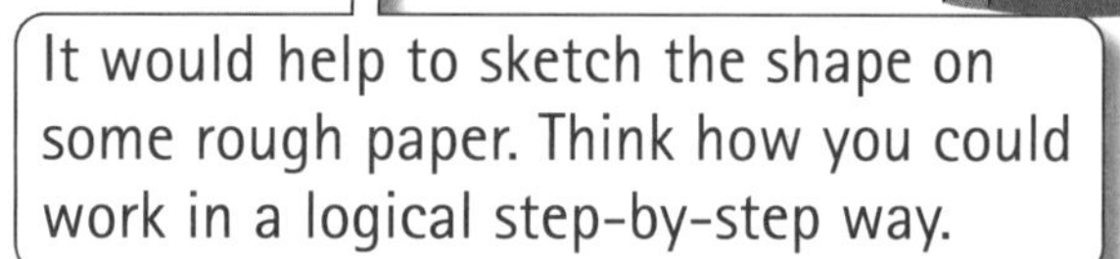

It would help to sketch the shape on some rough paper. Think how you could work in a logical step-by-step way.

3. Highlight key words and phrases.

"How many". We are going to need a total number of rectangles to be correct. Saying 'lots' won't be good enough!

4. Can you estimate an answer?

We can see 9 inside the big one straight away. That's 10. Let's say double that. 20?

5. What calculations do you need to do?

Work in a logical way using a table.
How many 1-unit rectangles are there?
How many 2-unit rectangles are there?
And so on...

6. What is the answer to your calculations? Show how you got your answer.

Number of units	1	2	3	4	5	6	7	8	9	10	Total
Number of rectangles	9	12	6	4	0	4	0	0	1	0	36

7. What is the answer to the original problem? Write it in full sentences.

We can see 36 rectangles in this shape.

8. Is your answer a sensible one?

It looks sensible because we worked in a step-by-step way. Our estimate was quite a long way out, but a logical approach has given us the correct answer.

Practice questions

Use the flow chart to help you to answer these questions about shape and space.

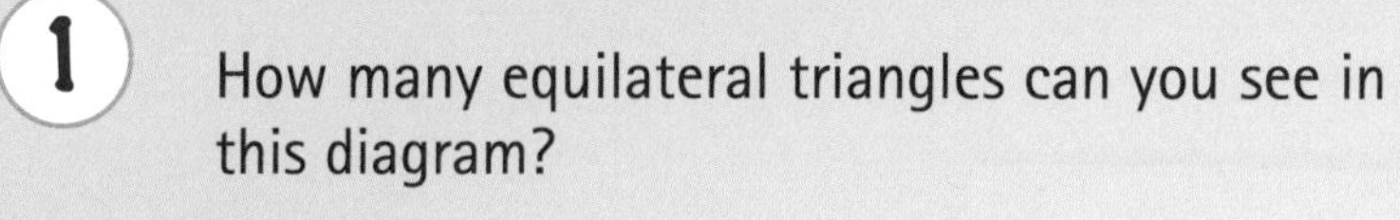

1. How many equilateral triangles can you see in this diagram?

Show your method.

2. How many squares can you count?

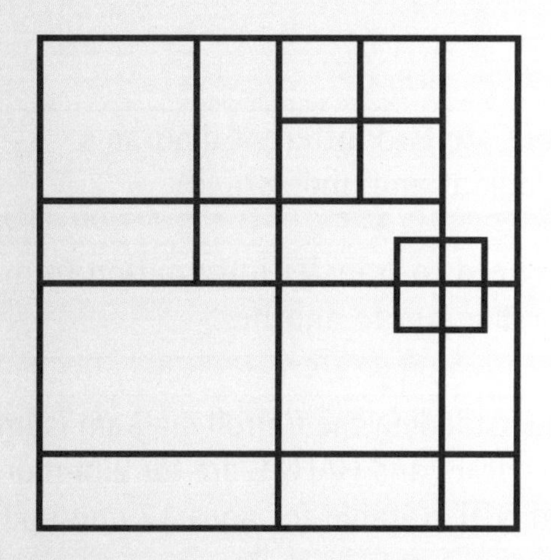

Show your method.

3. Imagine a dice and an open box that is just big enough to hold it.

How many ways can you fit the dice into the open box?

Show your method.

Solving data handling problems

Let's try a simple data handling problem.

Theo has carried out a survey of some popular computer games. Find *Gran Theft Skateboard*, *HALO 5* and *Wrestling Fest* in the Carroll diagram below. Write them in the correct place on the Venn diagram.

Suitable for 12 and under

1 player only

	Suitable for ages 12 and under	Not suitable for ages 12 and under
1 player only	Gran Theft Skateboard Speed Racer 2	Zombie Hunter Horror-shocker
2 or more players	Wrestling Fest	Car-jacker HALO 5

1. Read the question then read it again.
   There are two different diagrams to look at and understand.
2. Picture the words and numbers. What do they mean?
   We need to transfer information from one diagram to another.
3. Highlight key words and phrases.
   Understanding the Carroll diagram is important. Car-jacker and HALO 5 are for 2 or more players and NOT suitable for ages 12 and under.
4. Can you estimate an answer?
   No, it would be a wild guess.
5. What calculations do you need to do?
   No calculations here. We need to put three games in the correct positions on the Venn diagram.
6. What is the answer to your calculations? Show how you got your answer.
   Wrestling Fest is for ages 12 and under but needs 2 or more players, so it goes in the left hand circle. *Gran Theft Skateboard* is for 12 and under AND 1 player only, so it goes where the 2 circles meet., *HALO 5* doesn't fit in either category so goes outside both circles.
7. What is the answer to the original problem? Write it in full sentences.
   Now we can fill in the Venn diagram with the three games in the correct places.
8. Is your answer a sensible one?
   After double-checking what we have written and where, it is a sensible answer.

Practice questions

Use the flow chart help you to answer these data handling questions.

1

I am trying to find a number. It is a multiple of 7. It is an even number. It is less than 25. What is the number?

Complete this table to help you find the answer.

Multiples of 7 less than 25	Even numbers less than 25

Show your method.

My number is a square number. It has two digits but is less than 50. It is divisible by 3. What is my number?

Clue: Try using a table like the one in question 1.

Show your method.

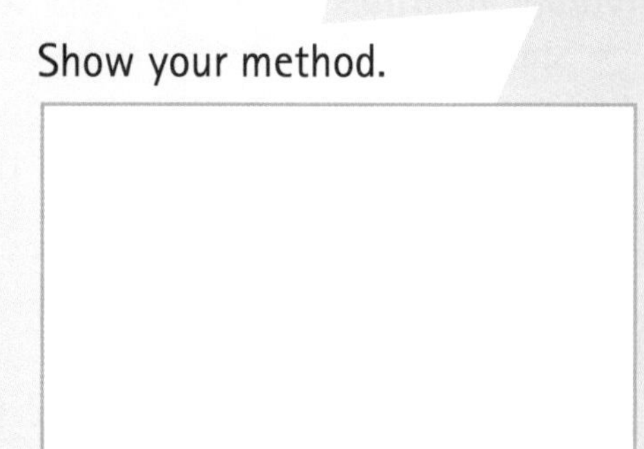

3

Six villages are joined together by a bus route. The bus goes from A and back to A.

It visits each of the other towns once.
How many different bus routes are there?

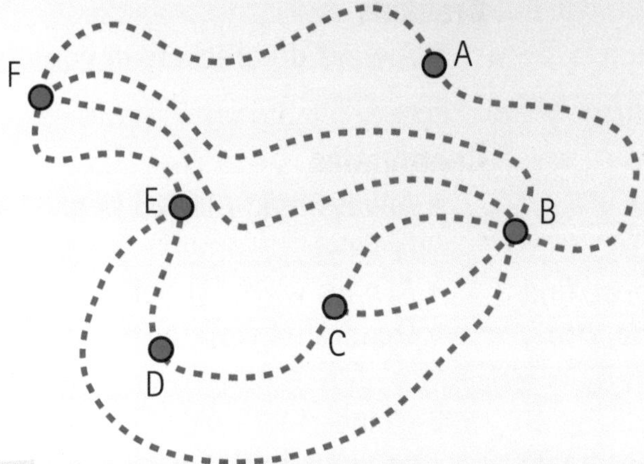

Show your method.

4

Isobel, Ollie, William, Sam and Kay all meet at school. Each child shakes hands with every other child. How many handshakes are there altogether? Use a diagram to help you.
Show your method.

KEY FACTS

The Number System and Calculations

Multiplying decimals by 10, 100 and 1000

- Shuffle numbers to the left.
- Shuffle numbers to the left once when × 10, twice when × 100 and three times when × 1000.

Dividing decimals by 10, 100 and 1000

- Shuffle numbers to the right.
- Shuffle numbers to the right once when ÷ by 10, twice when ÷ by 100, and three times when ÷ by 1000.

Negative numbers

- Integers are just whole numbers.
- When counting from negative up to positive or positive down to negative, **remember to count 0!**
- When counting on a number line, count to the right when adding, count to the left when subtracting.

Decimals to two places

- When rounding, remember 5 is up!
  6.785 = 6.79

Reducing a fraction to its simplest form

- To reduce a fraction to its simplest form, find a common factor which you can divide into the numerator and the denominator.
  For example, $\frac{3 \div 3}{9 \div 3} = \frac{1}{3}$

Calculating a fraction or percentage

- Remember as many percentage/fraction equivalents as you can:

  50% = $\frac{1}{2}$ 25% = $\frac{1}{4}$ 75% = $\frac{3}{4}$

  33% = nearly $\frac{1}{3}$ 66% = nearly $\frac{2}{3}$

Multiplication and division (with decimal points)

- × and ÷ are opposites.
- Always estimate first. It will help you to get the decimal point in the right place if one is needed.

Checking your answers

- Inverse means opposite!
- Check addition by subtraction – and vice versa.
- Check division by multiplication – and vice versa.
- Use 'friendly numbers' when estimating: 2, 5, 10, etc.

Simple formulae

- **Talk** through the formula in your head. It will make it easier.

Brackets

- Always do brackets in equations first.

Coordinates

- Always read ALONG (x axis) and then UP (y axis).
- Always write (x) before (y) – (x, y).
- Quadrants work **anti-clockwise.**

3 o'clock to 12 o'clock	= Quadrant 1
12 o'clock to 9 o'clock	= Quadrant 2
9 o'clock to 6 o'clock	= Quadrant 3
6 o'clock to 3 o'clock	= Quadrant 4

Measures, Shape and Space

2D shapes

- Pentagon
  Pentagons have FIVE sides.
  Regular pentagons have FIVE EQUAL SIDES.

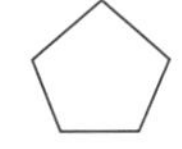

- Parallelogram
  A parallelogram is a RECTANGLE THAT HAS BEEN PUSHED OVER.
  Remember the opposite sides are the same length but parallel.

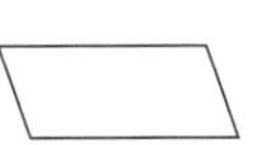

- Isosceles and scalene triangles
  An isosceles triangle has TWO EQUAL SIDES AND TWO EQUAL ANGLES.
  Picture an isosceles triangle as an arrow!
  A scalene triangle has THREE SIDES OF DIFFERENT LENGTHS and THREE ANGLES OF DIFFERENT sizes.
  When picturing a scalene triangle, think of SCALING A MOUNTAIN that has an easy way up or a more difficult side to climb!

Angles

- Acute angle = 0–89°
- Right angle = 90°
- Obtuse angle = 91–179°
- Straight line = 180°
- Reflex angle = 181–359°
- Angles around a POINT always add up to 360° (a complete turn).
- The angles of a TRIANGLE always add up to 180°.

Symmetries

- When drawing reflections, remember to keep the correct distance from the mirror line.

Metric and imperial conversions (approximate)

- 1 litre = 1.8 pints
- 1 kilogram = 2.2 lbs (pounds)
- 1 pound = 0.454 kg
- 1 mile = 1.6 km
- 5 miles = 8 km
- 1 foot = 30 cm
- 1 metre = 3 feet 3 inches
- 1 inch = 2.5 cm

Estimating measures

- Milli = very small
- Centi = small
- Kilo = big

Area of a rectangle

- Area of a rectangle = length (L) × width (W)
- Area is always units squared (cm^2, m^2, mm^2)

Handling Data

Pictograms

- With pictograms PICTURE = NUMBER
  e.g. 🍦 = 20 ice creams (= 10 ice creams

Mean, median, range, mode

- Mean = sum of all numbers divided by number of numbers
- Median = middle number in sequence (always write down in order first)
- Range = difference between highest and lowest number
- Mode = most common value

Charts and graphs

- Be careful and accurate. Use a sharp pencil.
- Pie charts are good for percentages, fractions or decimals.

Probability scale

- Always goes from 0 to 1 (you need fractions/decimals here).

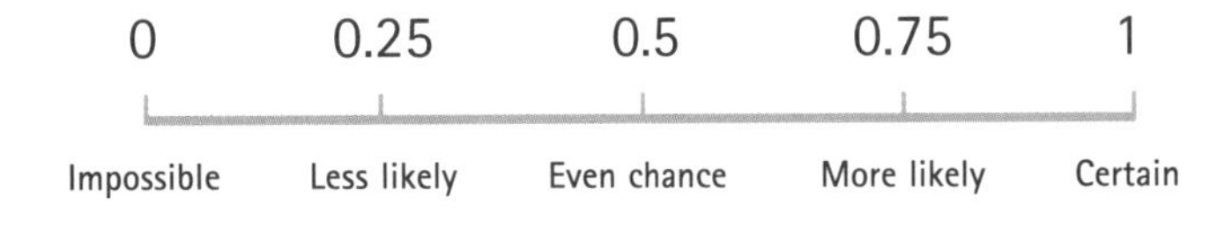

Test techniques

Before a test

1. When you revise, try revising a 'little and often' rather than in long sessions.
2. Learn your multiplication facts up to 10×10 so that you can recall them instantly. These are your tools for performing your calculations.
3. Revise with a friend. You can encourage and learn from each other.
4. Get a good night's sleep the night before.
5. Be prepared – bring your own pens and pencils and wear a watch to check the time as you go.

During a test

1. Don't rush the first few questions. These tend to be quite straightforward, so don't make any silly mistakes.
2. As you know by now, READ THE QUESTION THEN READ IT AGAIN.
3. If you get stuck, don't linger on the same question – move on! You can come back to it later.
4. Never leave a multiple choice question. Make an educated guess if you really can't work out the answer.
5. Check to see how many marks a question is worth. Have you 'earned' those marks with your answer?
6. Check your answers. You can use the inverse method or the rounding method. Does your answer look correct?
7. Be aware of the time. After 20 minutes, check to see how far you have got.
8. Try to leave a couple of minutes at the end to read through what you have written.
9. Always show your method. You may get a mark for showing you have gone through the correct procedure even if your answer is wrong.
10. Don't leave any questions unanswered. In the two minutes you have left yourself at the end, make an educated guess at the questions you really couldn't do.

The National Tests

Key facts

- The Key Stage 2 National Tests (or SATs) take place in the middle of May in Year 6. You will be tested on Maths, English and Science.
- The tests take place in your school and will be marked by examiners – not your teacher!
- You will get your results in July, two months after you take the tests.
- Individual test scores are not made public but a school's combined scores are published in what are commonly known as league tables.

The Maths National Tests

You will take three tests in Maths:

Mental Maths Test – This test will be played to you on a cassette. You will have to answer the questions mentally within 5, 10 or 15 seconds. This test will take about 20 minutes.

Test A – The non-calculator test. This test requires quick answers on a test paper. You will not be able to use a calculator but should show any working you do.

Test B – This test allows you to use a calculator and includes problems that will take you longer to solve.

Don't forget!

Using and Applying Mathematics – There will be more questions testing how you use and apply your mathematical knowledge in different situations. This includes: knowing which is the important information in the questions; how to check your results; describing things mathematically using common symbols and diagrams; and explaining your reasons for conclusions that you make.

Many of the questions include elements of Using and Applying Mathematics but we have also added extra pages with specific questions designed to help you succeed in this new area of testing: pages 48 to 57.

You might be asked to explain your answers and also write possible answers. Remember, always show your method.

Answers

Page 8 – Decimal notation and negative numbers
1) 7 pounds and 42 pence 2) 14 pounds and 28 pence 3) 53 pounds and 71 pence
4) 109 pounds and 86 pence 5) 426 pounds and 19 pence (b) is colder

Page 9 – Subtraction
1) 71 2) 167 3) 146 4) 138 5) 164 6) 99

Page 10 – 2, 3, 4, 5 and 10 times table
1) 2 2) 7 3) 70 4) 9 5) 5
6) 14 7) 8 8) 80 9) 6 10) 32
11) 5 12) 5 13) 6 14) 1 15) 7

Page 12 – Equivalent Fractions
Circled marbles = $\frac{2}{3}$ Not circled marbles = $\frac{1}{3}$

Answers will vary e.g. $\frac{2}{8} = \frac{1}{4}$ $\frac{1}{3} = \frac{2}{6}$

Page 13 – Classifying 3D and 2D shapes

	Cone	Cylinder	Sphere	Cuboid	Triangular-based pyramid	Triangular prism
Number of faces	2	3	1	6	4	5
Number of edges	1	2	0	12	6	9
Number of vertices	1	0	0	8	4	6

Page 14 – Tables and lists
1) Enya 2) Jessica and Enya 3) Jessica and Thomas

Page 15 – Bar charts and pictograms
1) tuna mayonnaise 2) 7 3) 18

Page 17 – Multiplying and dividing by 10 and 100
1) 650 2) 10 3) 100 4) 42 200
5) 17 6) 10 7) 10 8) 70

Page 18 – Short addition
1) 8493 2) 899 3) 2080 4) 11 979

Page 19 – Short subtraction
1) 7951 2) 6188 3) 7960 4) 2525

Page 20 – Decimals
1) 15.11 2) 123.3 km 3) £15.92 4) 8.56 5) 1.28 6) 38.84 km

Page 21 – Decimals
1) 1.77, 7.87, 8.7, 8.87, 18.28 2) 2.55 km, 5.22 km, 25.52 km, 55.2 km
3) 9.224, 9.242, 9.424, 9.442, 9.99 4) 0.077, 0.73, 0.734, 0.773

Page 22 – Short multiplication
1) 2550 2) 2852 3) 1995 4) 2534 5) 6957 6) 5112

Page 23 – Short division
1) 48 2) 78 r1 3) 297 4) 91 r 6

Page 24 – Recognising proportions of a whole
1) dog 2) 30

Page 25 – Recognising proportions of a whole

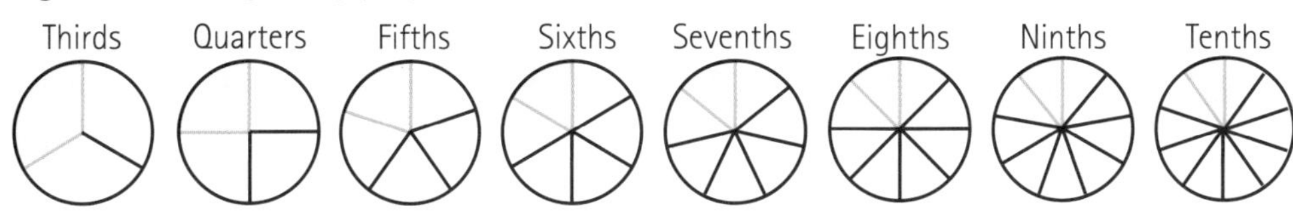

Page 26 – Number patterns

1) 0 and 10. Rule is 'add 5'.
2) 34 and 85. Rule is 'add 17'
3) 141, 72 and 49. Rule is 'subtract 23'.

Page 27 – Number patterns

1) 32: 1, 2, 4, 8, 16, 32
2) 60: 1, 2, 3, 4, 5, 6, 10, 12, 15, 20, 30, 60
3) 42: 1, 2, 3, 6, 7, 14, 21, 42
4) 80: 1, 2, 4, 5, 8, 10, 16, 20, 40, 80

Prime numbers 2, 3, 5, 7, 11, 13, 17, 19, 23, 29, 31, 37, 41, 43, 47, 53, 59, 61, 67, 71, 73, 79, 83, 89, 91, 97

Page 28 – Checking your answers

1) 457 check $457 + 67 = 524$
2) 40 check $40 \times 4 = 160$
3) 6987 check $6987 + 897 = 7884$
4) 45 check $45 \times 50 = 2250$

1) 7557 Rough answer = $700 \times 10 = 7000$
2) 283 Rough answer $400 - 100 = 300$
3) 26 Rough answer $460 \div 20 = 23$

Page 29 – Checking your answers

1011 / In his first calculation, Billy put 112 instead of 12 into his calculator. $435 \times 112 = 48{,}720$

Page 30 – Using coordinates

1) (4, 1); (2, 5) and (6, 5)
2) (a) Phantom Hill (b) Carnage Cliff (c) Pirate Point

Page 31 – Using coordinates

Answers will vary

Page 32 – 3D shapes – making models

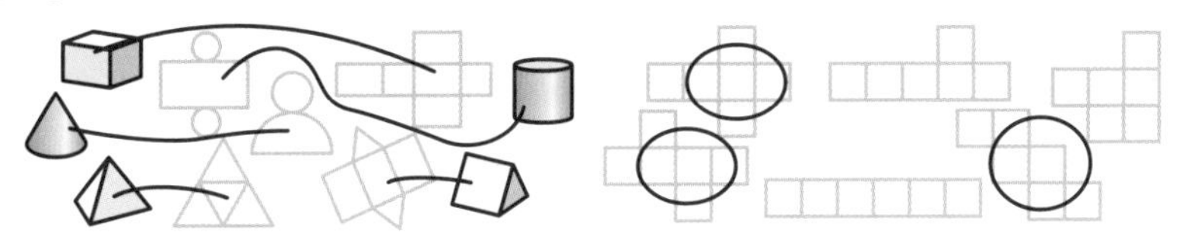

Page 33 – 3D shapes – making models

First example needs 8 blocks to complete the cuboid
Second example needs 8 blocks to complete the cuboid

Page 34 – 2D shapes

Answers will vary

Page 35 – 2D shapes

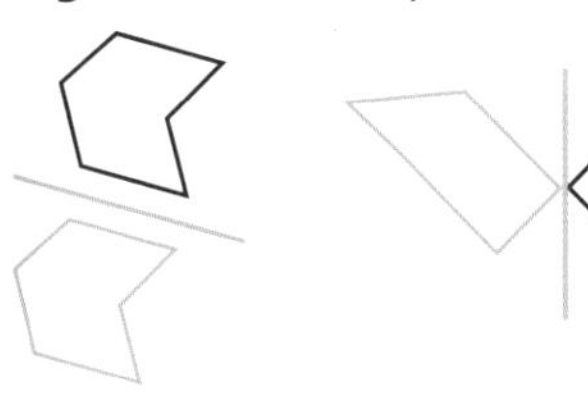

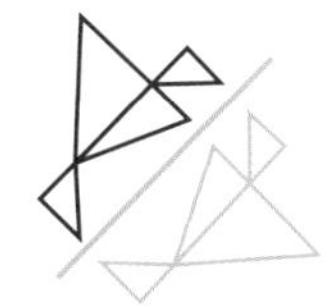

Page 38 – Measures

1) Your foot, DVD case
2) Glass of milk, can of cola
3) Scales
4) Ruler
5) Answers will vary. Use chart to check answers.

Page 40 – Grouping data

1) 2
2) 6
3) 6 – 10
4) 12
5) No they didn't

Page 42 – Finding the range

19 341 books

Page 43 – Finding the mode
Mode = 2

Page 44 – Line graphs
1) June, 8500 surfboards were sold. 2) February and March 3) July and August
4) June, July and August 5) Could be bought as Christmas presents.

Page 45 – Line graphs
1) 5 2) August and September 3) 3 places

Page 47 – Using simple formulae
1) £9 2) 5 3) £4
A = (J × 9) + 3

Page 51 – Solving number problems
1) The candles were £18
2) The fondue set was £25
3) Baz and Gaz shortchange ' Eadcase by 10p so 'Eadcase 'Arry will do one of two things, depending on his mood:
(a) Let Baz and Gaz be the first to 'try-out' the new butchers' block and fondue set.
(b) Make them put all the flat-pack furniture together and redecorate the hideout in a nice shade of peach.

Page 53 – Solving measures problems

1) 1600 cups of punch 2) 1968 m or 1.968 km 3) Billy Biceps lifts 201.5 kg 4) 8072 litres
5) 24 revolutions per ride 6) 4.95 kg or 4950 grams of food

Page 55 – Solving shape and space problems

1) 27 2) 22 3) 24 ways

Page 56 – Solving data handling problems
Venn Diagram – flow chart

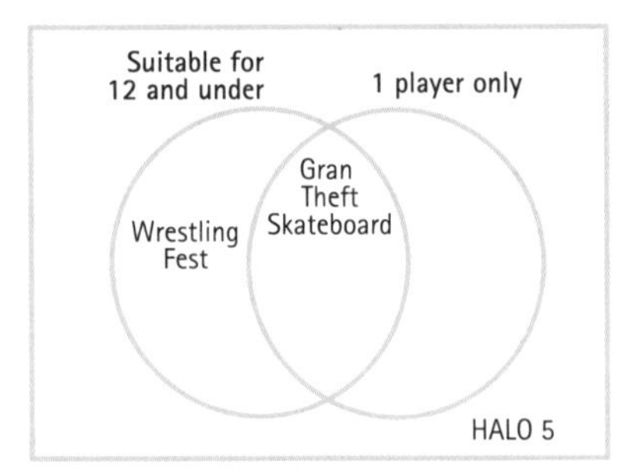

Page 57 – Solving data handling problems
1) Multiples of 7 = 7, 14, 21
Even numbers = 2, 4, 6, 8, 10, 12, 14, 16, 18, 20, 22, 24
The answer is 14

2) Square numbers = 16, 25, 36, 49
Two-digit numbers = 12, 15, 18, 21, 24, 27, 30, 33, 36, 39, 42, 45, 48
The answer is 36

3) A/B/C/D/E/F/A or the reverse of this are the only two solutions.

4) 10 handshakes

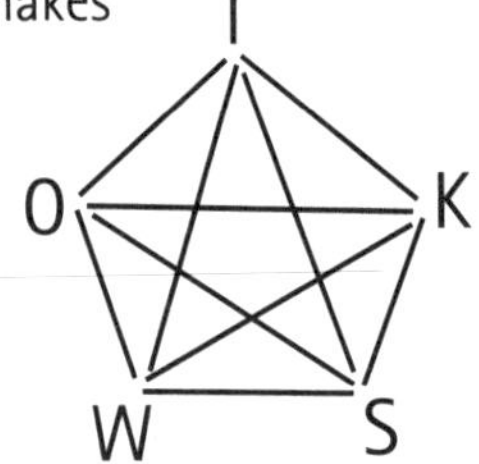